WRESTLING WITH THE PATRIARCHS

*W*RESTLING
with the
PATRIARCHS

Retrieving Women's Voices
in Preaching

Lee McGee
with Thomas H. Troeger

ABINGDON PRESS / Nashville

WRESTLING WITH THE PATRIARCHS:
RETRIEVING WOMEN'S VOICES IN PREACHING

Copyright © 1996 by Abingdon Press

This book is printed on acid-free, recycled paper.

Library of Congress Cataloging-in-Publication Data

McGee, Lee.
    Wrestling with the patriarchs : retrieving women's voices in
preaching / Lee McGee ; with Thomas H. Troeger.
        p.   cm. — (Abingdon preacher's library)
    Includes bibliographical references.
    ISBN 0-687-00621-X (pbk. : alk. paper)
    1. Preaching.   2. Women clergy.   3. Feminist theology.
I. Troeger, Thomas H., 1945–   .   II. Title.   III. Series.
BV4211.2.M35   1996
251'.0082—dc20   96-3017
                                                                       CIP

Scripture quotations, unless otherwise indicated, are from the New
Revised Standard Version Bible, copyright © 1989, by the Division of
Christian Education of the National Council of the Churches of
Christ in the United States of America.

96 97 98 99 00 01 02 03 04 05—10 9 8 7 6 5 4 3 2 1

MANUFACTURED IN THE UNITED STATES OF AMERICA

CONTENTS

ACKNOWLEDGMENTS

I BEGAN PONDERING GENDER ISSUES IN THE MINISTRY MANY years ago. In the mid-1960s, while a student at Yale Divinity School, I was encouraged by Professor James Dittes in a research project on the issues, themes, and patterns in the vocational development of women pastors. As has so often been true, Professor Dittes responded to my questions with interest, respect, and encouragement providing guidance intellectually and personally. I am so grateful for his continued role as mentor and friend in my life and work. The seeds of this book were first nourished by his wisdom.

Certainly, Tom Troeger, who has edited this book, stands in a very special role. His counsel has been invigorating, motivating, and sustaining. His sensitivity and skill as an editor are remarkable.

I have been blessed by the interest and encouragement of family and friends. I am most grateful to my sons, Kyle and Matthew, who never question the importance of this book or the capacity of their mother to write it. Such encouragement of my voice has been a wonderful gift from son to mother.

Friends and colleagues have commented on the ideas and themes of this book, and I am particularly grateful for my dear friend Flora Keshgegian. Special thanks go to Anne Hamilton, journalist, writer, and dear friend. Anne is the one who enabled me to try writing again after twenty-five years of absence from research following the onset of partial blindness in 1967. She coached me throughout the process of voice recovery as a writer.

Last but never least is the gratitude I feel for the many students who have served as research assistants and typists for this manuscript. Maggie Gatt, Dawn Detgen, Nicki Stipe, Susan Sprowls, Jim Tuite, Kirk Mylander, and Molly Crichton have done the hard work of research and have typed the countless revisions so essential to producing a book.

I offer special thanks to Evelyn Rodriguez of the Yale Divinity School staff for all the technical services she provided.

The College of Preachers in Washington, D.C., has played a significant part in the research into gender issues in the preaching and leadership of women in the church's ministry. Through conferences and consultations, the College of Preachers has provided resources for preachers and scholars in this era of collaboration in ministry for men and women.

Of singular importance in the writing of this book is the discussion of its ideas with colleagues in ministry—pastors, faculty, and students. Their interest and encouragement have sustained my inquiry over the years amidst the demands of my professional and personal life.

FOREWORD

WHEN I FIRST HEARD LEE MCGEE MAKE A PRESENTATION about welcoming women's voices in the pulpit, I looked around the room and saw lights go on in the faces of women and men alike. I felt the satisfying "aha!" that arises when we identify what we have dimly perceived but never fully named and described.

At the time I had been teaching preaching for sixteen years. I had observed how difficult it was for many women students to get in the pulpit and preach. Men also had their struggles, but the complexity and intensity of the struggle were consistently greater for women. I also had seen the amazing range of reactions to women preaching, from effusive praise to resistance and hostility. Men also drew varied responses, but again the complexity and intensity were greater in the case of women.

How were the women preachers to understand those things? Because they were responsible people, it was natural for them first to seek an explanation in themselves as individuals: What am *I* doing to make the creation of sermons such a consuming task? Why do I evoke such powerful reactions?

Although it never hurts to examine one's own performance, the repeated pattern of so many women's experience in the pulpit made it clear that something larger than purely individual reaction was involved. To illuminate that pattern, Lee McGee draws upon psychological studies about the development of women. She identifies the sources of their doubts about their own voices as preachers. She gathers data from preachers and listeners and draws a picture of the different ways that congregations perceive men and women in the pulpit. The result is a great clarification of the complex act of communication that transpires between a woman preacher and a congregation.

But Lee McGee does not stop with psychological and communications analyses. She places her work in the context of leading women in the history of the church. Instead of feeling that we are dealing with something entirely new, we realize that there are models and sources of wisdom from the past for nurturing more effective communication between women preachers and congregations.

Lee McGee concludes her work with a fully outlined course based on her theoretical, empirical, and historical work. The book not only gives us an "aha!" about our experience; it also provides a practical road map to direct women toward the realization of their authentic voice in the pulpit. In accomplishing this, McGee helps both preachers and the church to claim more completely two things: a healthier model of Christian community and a keener sense of what it means to live an incarnational faith.

The healthier community results from a willingness to face the differences in how women and men find their voices in the pulpit and how the different voices are received. It is often tempting to deny such differences for fear of the complexities that will arise once we acknowledge them. But denial does not change facts. It is far better to have the differences out in the open and to explore what they mean and what liabilities and possibilities they present. I think of a former woman student who was being interviewed for a pastoral position where a woman had never served before. When a member of the committee said, "It surely would feel different to have a woman in the pulpit," she responded, "Yes, it would feel different. Can you name some of the ways it would feel different for you?" There followed a helpful conversation because they faced the differences rather than pretended they did not exist. That is the kind of healthy, clarifying communication that Lee McGee's work makes possible.

Her theory and practice also remind us that preaching is an incarnational act. Preaching is not simply words on a page or words in the air. Preaching is the physical action of lung and voice, lips and face, posture and gesture. To say gender makes no difference is to forget that preaching is the truth of God coming through particular human beings, the fullness of who they are, which includes the preacher's identity as woman or man.

Through her affirmation of the incarnational character of preaching and her methods for moving beyond the distortions of gender bias, Lee McGee performs a gracious act of pastoral care that extends to women and men alike. Not burdened with the denial of our differences, we are freed to welcome women's voices in the pulpit with a hospitality that proclaims the gospel more fully: "There is no longer Jew or Greek, there is no longer slave or free, there is no longer male and female; for all of you are one in Christ Jesus" (Gal. 3:28).

T. H. T.

CHAPTER 1

Issues for Women Preachers

For me, the preaching experience is best conveyed in the image of God and Jacob wrestling. There is a combination of feelings, like a wound and a blessing. I'm never sure if I'm meeting an angel or a demon in the sermon preparation and delivery.

—A woman preacher

I HAVE BEEN ATTENTIVE TO WOMEN'S VOICES FOR AS LONG AS I can remember. The tone of my mother's voice let me know if it was going to be a good or bad day. So it surprises me when people cannot remember women's voices. I begin my discussion of voice retrieval in preaching classes by asking students to recall a woman who influenced them spiritually during childhood. I ask them: "Recall this woman's message spoken or unspoken. What did she teach you about God and about the world? What spiritual truth did she convey to you?" There is always silence as people ponder the questions. In a few minutes, the discussion begins.

One person says skeptically, "I couldn't think of a woman who influenced me spiritually."

"Me, either," another chimes in.

"How many of you couldn't recall any such woman?"
I ask. About a third of the hands go up.

Someone pipes up, "I couldn't remember, but finally,
I did. I didn't think there was anyone, but then I thought
of . . ."

And so it goes. The group begins to remember—one
memory triggers another. As we remember, the voices of
women are heard. In time, it is evident to the class that
indeed many women have conveyed important spiritual
truths. The voices of those women, which were lost, are
retrieved and heard anew.

This book will seek to examine the process of losing
and retrieving women's voices, past and present. We will
explore the factors that influence the voice loss—factors
that affect women in preaching and factors that affect
the hearing of women's voices in congregations.

It is important to define the terms I use in this book.
I use the term *voice* to refer to the concept that has been
put forth by the researchers working on the Harvard
University and Stone Center Collaborative Study of the
Psychological Development of Women and Girls. That
research examines statements made by girls relating to
gender, reality, and relationships during the passage
from childhood into adolescence. A significant decrease
in "I know" statements is noted in girls age eleven to
fourteen. Such "I know" statements indicate an internal, personal security regarding perceptions and knowledge. This decrease has been labeled *loss of voice* by the
researchers in early reporting on the study. Thus, I speak
of a woman's *voice, loss of voice,* and *retrieval of voice*
in this book. These may be new terms and concepts for
the reader. This book examines this research and its
implications for preaching and preachers. I believe
understanding the concept of voice will prove of great
value for the preaching ministry just as it has for the
fields of education and psychology.

To be a faithful woman preacher requires a multidisciplinary effort. In this book I draw upon four disciplines to understand the sources and the conflicts that are involved in women finding their authentic voices as preachers:

1. Developmental psychology
2. Behavioral psychology
3. Church history
4. Spirituality

I show how psychological insights about the development and suppression of women's voices illumine the history of women in the church, particularly the history of women who have been named saints or who are esteemed for the richness of their theological and spiritual insight.

I believe this broad-based approach will help women preachers to see that the challenges and, perhaps, difficulties they experience as preachers are a function of something much larger than only their individual experience. These difficulties in fact arise out of the nature of our culture, its understandings of power, its expectations of women, and the religious legacy of the past.

Early in my ministry I became intrigued by the preaching event and the response it provoked in the listener. Several experiences challenged my understanding of preaching. To begin with, I was surprised by the intensity of my anxiety as I prepared to preach. I spent hours in thought and study. I prepared manuscripts—wrote and rewrote—ending up with far too much material. I excised whole sections, a process I have come to call "winnowing." I learned that, for the twenty-four hours before preaching, my entire body, mind, and spirit were focused on the upcoming preaching event. "Does everyone suffer this intense anxiety?" I wondered. Many

seemed to do so, especially women. Why did it consume
me so? I pondered this question and realized that, unlike
teaching, in preaching my soul and body were the vehicles of communication: starkly, frighteningly visible—
naked for all to see. They were not someone else's
words. They were my words, my ideas, and I presumed
to present them in relation to God's Word. No wonder
my terror!

Another thought-provoking experience involved the
reaction of others to my preaching. I began preaching
regularly in 1965 when there were very few women
preachers. So it was a new experience for most congregations to hear a woman preach. Reactions varied. Most
startling was the wonder people expressed that I could
preach at all. Breathlessly, a woman would greet me at
the back of the church. "That was a wonderful sermon!"
she would exclaim, as if she could hardly believe it. At
first I attributed it to lack of experience with women
preachers, but as such reactions continued over the
years, I realized that most people assumed women could
not preach. They seemed to feel it was impossible for
women to preach well. That feeling was even more evident in comments such as, "I could hear you," uttered
with wonder, as if it were a most remarkable phenomenon. Another frequent response, usually from men, was,
"Well, that was very good," stated in a soft, patronizing
voice denoting surprise, as if a child had accomplished
something beyond her years.

In those years, I discovered that the content of the sermon had very little relationship to the reaction of the
hearer. One friend explained, "It's such a powerful experience for them to *see* you in the pulpit and discover you
can preach that they can't get beyond the experience to
hear you." This response was illustrated when I
preached in a Roman Catholic church on the role of
women in the church. My visit was quite controversial,

since Roman Catholic women are not allowed to preach. My sermon was critical and challenging. Within moments, hearers gushed, "That was wonderful!" "Great sermon!" I was startled. Why were they not angry? At me? At the church? Had they heard my sermon? I could understand their reaction only as a statement of their wonder that I could stand in a pulpit and make sense. The hearers seemed to presume that a woman preacher had very little capacity to deliver an instructive sermon (i.e., a woman preacher is not worth listening to).

Such experiences repeated themselves too often to be discounted. I began to analyze their meaning. I compared notes with other women preachers and heard similar accounts. I sought out opportunities to hear women preach. I wondered, What is distinctive about the preaching of women and the hearing of women's voices?

I considered my own evolution as a preacher. Initially, my preaching imitated the preachers I admired—all men. My preaching was filled with scholarship. I realized I had learned to preach from role models primarily rather than books or instruction. I realized that all of my role models were male. How could I find my own voice and style as a preacher? What I did was to keep preaching and adapting my style. I decided that preaching was oral communication with a large group and, therefore, a new medium for me.

I drew for myself an analogy of learning to swim. Learning to transport my body in water as a swimmer was similar to learning to use my body and voice in a sanctuary. I was learning to express myself in a new medium. Over time I weaned myself from a full manuscript to an outline for preaching. I realized that a sermon is not written communication but *spoken* communication. It is like—but is not—conversation. Preaching is a communication event between one person and a group of individuals in a very large space. The persona of the preacher is essential to the communication.

Throughout my development as a preacher, various questions kept recurring, and I found myself pondering the following issues:

❖ What is the nature of women's preaching?
❖ How would the congregation, the hearers, describe women's preaching?
❖ Is women's preaching distinct from the preaching of men?

In 1979, I was part of the leadership team for a conference for women preachers—lay and ordained—of all denominations. The conference was sponsored by the College of Preachers in Washington, D.C., a nationally recognized educational center. About thirty women from churches throughout the United States participated. Prior to attending the conference, each woman circulated a simple questionnaire in her congregation, asking people to describe men's preaching and women's preaching. The goal was to do some informal data gathering that we could review during the conference. The results were fascinating. The questionnaire and the responses are presented and discussed fully in the next chapters, as is an examination of the preaching ministry of women. Some of the questions that will be discussed are the following:

❖ Is there a distinctiveness to the preaching of women?
❖ Does the listener hear women's voices and women's preaching differently from men's preaching?
❖ Is there a culturally informed resistance to the voices of women within the hearer? Within the congregation?

These questions are examined through data gathered from women preachers, women seminarians, and the men and women of numerous congregations. However, these questions lead to a more fundamental inquiry, which is, What does it mean to be a faithful woman preacher? I suggest it means being engaged in hearing women's voices, past and present. It means using one's voice in dialogue with God and with others. It means being engaged in a retrieval of women's voices in the past, the present, and the future. It is my conviction that this requires a multidisciplinary effort. It means drawing on the resources of developmental psychology, behavioral psychology, history, and spirituality.

This book represents an effort to present the voices of women themselves. The comments of women preachers provide valuable perspective about how women view preaching, how the preaching of women develops, and how it is received. Information was gathered, also, from conferences of women preachers in 1979 and 1994 at the College of Preachers, where women preachers discussed their preaching in light of years of congregational experience.

This book also discusses voice use in women in the church—lay and ordained. It examines *voice loss, risks to voice,* and *voice retrieval,* and presents a voice retrieval process that was developed from seminars for women in church leadership, lay and ordained. With so many resources, the work of integrating them has been a formidable and rewarding challenge.

This difficult integrative task exemplifies what lies at the heart of the issues of voice use in women and how women are heard in the church. Women listen to and value many voices from all parts of their world. I believe a woman listens so well to others and seeks others' voices so effectively that she may not appreciate and develop her own voice. Or a woman may believe that she should withhold her voice in deference to or consideration for others. Thus, a conflict arises in women over the use of voice. The conflict for women preachers is this: How do I balance the private and communal perspectives in my voice? Or put another way, How do I find a voice that is faithful to the community and authentic to my own identity?

In addition to her internal conflict, the woman preacher speaks to a community that is ambivalent, either consciously or unconsciously, about hearing her voice. Women often speak to communities that are unaccustomed to hearing women preach and resistant to the new and "different" perspectives of women. No wonder it is difficult for women to speak and to be heard. It has been so for this writer.

CHAPTER 2

Gender and Preaching

But on the first day of the week, at early dawn, they came to the tomb, taking the spices that they had prepared. They found the stone rolled away from the tomb, but when they went in, they did not find the body. While they were perplexed about this, suddenly two men in dazzling clothes stood beside them. The women were terrified and bowed their faces to the ground, but the men said to them, "Why do you look for the living among the dead? He is not here, but has risen. Remember how he told you, while he was still in Galilee, that the Son of Man must be handed over to sinners, and be crucified, and on the third day rise again." Then they remembered his words, and returning from the tomb, they told all this to the eleven and to all the rest. Now it was Mary Magdalene, Joanna, Mary the mother of James, and the other women with them who told this to the apostles. But these words seemed to them an idle tale, and they did not believe them.

—Luke 24:1-11

IN THE PREVIOUS CHAPTER I PRESENTED SOME OF THE EXPERI-ences and resources that have shaped this inquiry into the distinctive nature of women's preaching. What began as curious interest became a long-term inquiry into gender issues in preaching. This inquiry was pursued in conferences, seminars, and classroom discussions. This chapter deals with the issues and data that emerged.

We begin our examination of women's preaching by hearing from women preachers themselves. Comments are taken from personal interviews, classes, and seminars. Women clergy and seminarians have raised the following questions as relevant to their preaching ministry:

What is the nature of women's preaching?

❖ What are the characteristics of women's preaching?
❖ What internal issues are raised within women as they approach the preaching task? (For example, how do women preachers feel about the preaching task? How do women preachers understand the preaching task?)

What is the response to women's preaching?

❖ Does the hearer hear women's preaching differently from the preaching of men?
❖ Does the gender of the hearer affect his or her understanding or hearing?
❖ Is there a culturally informed resistance to the preaching of women? Is such resistance present in the hearer? Is it present in the congregation? Is it present in the seminary?
❖ Are women aware of potential resistance to their preaching?
❖ Do women make efforts to defuse the resistance to their preaching by altering the content or delivery of sermons consciously or unconsciously?

In this chapter we address these issues using data and narrative commentary gathered from a wide community of women preachers and church leaders.

Little research exists on women's preaching. In 1979,

the College of Preachers in Washington, D.C., hosted a conference for women preachers. Approximately thirty women preachers from all over the U.S. gathered for a week to work together to improve their preaching. I was part of the leadership team for the conference. Recognizing the need for data on the preaching of women, the leadership team built informal data gathering into the conference. Each participant was asked to gather data from her congregation regarding characteristics of the preaching of women and characteristics of the preaching of men. About thirty congregations were surveyed with a total of approximately 150 responses.

Congregation members were asked to:

1. List the characteristics of the preaching of men.
2. List the characteristics of the preaching of women.
3. Offer additional comments.

The responses were gathered and summarized under the categories of preaching content, delivery, and style. They were also listed in order of frequency of response so that the first word in a list was the word most frequently cited by respondents. The results appear in table 1 on page 26.

The words and phrases that occurred most frequently are listed. This data confirmed my suspicion that there is a perceived distinctiveness to women's preaching.

In 1979, both men and women were perceived as undertaking challenging issues. Men were seen as dealing with the abstract and women with the practical or down-to-earth aspects of the issues. Men were described as dealing more with intellectual content and women with more emotional or experiential content.

In delivery, male preachers were described as controlled and female preachers as animated. A very interesting point in the data is the description of the speaking voice. Men's voices were variously described as rich, strong, full, and loud. Women's voices were described as expressive, yet hard to hear. The phrase "hard to hear" seems, at face value, to address audibility, but one wonders if it is an unconscious reference to a resistance to women's voices.

The 1979 data confirmed the importance of nonverbal factors in communication, such as appearance and demeanor, which communication experts assert again and again. In this data, the sermon delivery of men was related to physical size and strength in responses such as bigger and strong. Women, on the other hand, were described as solicitous, hesitant, and apologetic in sermon delivery. This particular description of the sermon delivery of women is of particular interest because these are the same words researchers report women and girls use to express ambivalence and fear about voice use.

Congregations in 1979 perceived sharp differences between male and female preachers in relation to style. Men were perceived as formal; women as informal. Men were seen as forceful; women apologetic. Men were labeled rational, and women were labeled personal. Men were perceived as authoritarian, and women were perceived as ingratiating. These sharp contrasts prove informative as we examine what women say about their feelings as they come to the preaching task, and as they deliberate about the risks of using their voices.

Certainly, the 1979 data reveal definite perceived differences in the preaching of men and women. These gender differences relate to content, delivery, and style of preaching. These perceived gender differences appear significant. Several differences in voice were described.

A similar questionnaire was administered through a conference for women preachers held in 1994, fifteen years later. This time, the responses came from approximately twenty-five congregations, with more than 250 questionnaires being received and analyzed. This time, an equal number of laymen and laywomen were given questionnaires in an attempt to track gender differences in the hearers as well as the preachers. The responses were summarized again, under the headings of content, delivery, and style. They were also listed in order of frequency in which they were cited. The most frequently cited word topped the list. (See table 2 on page 27.)

This small informal survey of predominantly Episcopal congregations across the U.S. confirmed again that there is a perceived distinction between the preaching of men and women. The same words and phrases occurred regularly in the responses from both men and women. Thus, this research indicates that the gender of the *hearer* does not significantly affect the way the preaching of men and women is perceived.

The 1994 data on perceived gender differences showed somewhat more common ground for the preaching of men and women than the 1979 data indicated. Women and men were characterized as thought-provoking, relevant, and biblical in their preaching content. However, many differences were still evident. Words like knowledgeable, scholarly, and informative described men's preaching content while women's preaching was described as personal and innovative.

In delivery, both male and female preachers were perceived as inspirational. However, men were considered more forceful in delivery. Women were characterized as evoking emotion as well as being direct in their delivery. Men were seen as persuasive and motivating, a seeming reference to moving the hearer mentally, perhaps evoking action as well. Again, speaking voice was noted with men characterized as louder while women were characterized as clear and sincere in delivery.

Perceived gender differences in style were quite divergent in the 1994 data. Men were described as distant and

Table 1

Perceived Gender Differences in Preaching
1980

MALE	*FEMALE*
CONTENT	*CONTENT*
— Intellectual	— Down-to-earth
— Theological	— Emotional
— Jargon	— Personal
— Hard questions	— Experiential
— Abstract	— Life issues
— Traditional and male illustrations	— No point
	— Too personal
DELIVERY	*DELIVERY*
— Confident	— Solicitous
— Controlled	— Inviting
— Voice-rich	— Apologetic
— Strong	— Hesitant
— Bigger	— Animated
	— Hard to hear
	— Expressive
	— Warm
STYLE	*STYLE*
— Formal	— Informal
— Forceful	— Warm
— Rational	— Personal
— Organized	— Apologetic
— Authoritarian	— Ingratiating
— Remote	

Responses listed in order of frequency. Data gathered by participants for the conferences, "Women and Preaching," The College of Preachers, Washington, D.C., 1979, 1980.

Table 2

Perceived Gender Differences in Preaching
1994

MALE	FEMALE
CONTENT	*CONTENT*
— Knowledgeable — Scholarly/academic — Biblical — Relevant — Thought-provoking — Informative — Issue-oriented	— Biblical — Relevant — Thought-provoking — Personal — Focused — Innovative
DELIVERY	*DELIVERY*
— Forceful — Inspirational — Louder — Persuasive — Motivating	— Direct — Evokes emotion — Inspirational — Less forceful — Clear/easy to understand — Sincere
STYLE	*STYLE*
— Authoritative — Less personal — Sincere — Distant — Formal — Boring — Dynamic	— Personal — Sensitive — Caring — Compassionate — Relational — Maternal/nurturing

Responses listed in order of frequency. Data gathered by participants in the conference: "Women Proclaiming," The College of Preachers, Washington, D.C., 1994.

less personal while women were rated as highly personal and relational. Men were perceived as having an authoritative, formal style compared to women's nurturing, caring, and compassionate style.

There appears to be less divergence in the perceived gender differences in the 1994 survey as compared to the 1979 survey. In addition, women's preaching is described in more positive, receptive tones and words than in the earlier study. Does the hearer feel a greater emotional response, perhaps even a stronger relationship to a woman preacher than a man preacher? This issue of relationship between preacher and hearer is relevant to the concepts presented in the next chapters on voice loss and voice retrieval. Hearers appear to register a stronger feeling response to women preaching than to men. Words dealing with feelings and emotional response to the preacher are noticeably absent in the characterization of men's preaching.

Do women preachers attend to relationship in their preaching content and/or in their preaching style? Does the content of a woman's preaching convey to the listener that human relationships are very important and that she seeks a positive relationship to the hearer? These questions arise as one surveys this data.

Having examined the nature of women's preaching and responses to it, I sought to examine the internal dynamics women preachers experience as they approach the preaching task.

My interviews indicate that women do approach the preaching task with a significant emotional reaction. Numerous women acknowledged that the preaching task evoked strong and often uncomfortable feelings such as "anxiety," "fear," "self-consciousness," "excitement," and "dread." Do these reactions reveal a greater sensitivity to the preacher-congregation relationship? Do the emotional reactions of women preachers represent performance anxiety or, perhaps, the unfamiliarity of the role of pastor/preacher? Do women preachers have less self-confidence or lower self-esteem, as some seminary professors have concluded?

Women seminarians characterized the task of sermon preparation and delivery as follows:

> Preaching is intense for me.
>
> The preaching experience is best conveyed by the image of God and Jacob wrestling. There is a combination of feelings, like a wound and a blessing. I'm never sure if I'm meeting an angel or a demon in the sermon preparation and delivery.
>
> How do I stay connected to people and speak the truth? That is my issue.
>
> My personal experience bumps right up against the experience of preaching to *men* and women. I have been exposed to critical men consistently, so I expect to be criticized.

This last student was asked, "What happens when you get a positive response? Are you able to hear it?"

"Sometimes," the student responded.

The last exchange reveals the complexity of this woman's emotional perspective on preaching. She has indicated that previous experiences in childhood and adulthood inform her response to the preaching task. Such comments are not unusual in preaching seminars.

One discussion with a group of women preachers with long experience in preaching was particularly revealing. They confirmed their own anxiety in sermon preparation. They confirmed that they worried about how sermon content would be received by members of the congregation. When these women preachers were asked, "Does the preaching anxiety ease as you get to know the congregation better, after a period of months or years?" they responded, "Oh, no, it gets worse the better you know them because you know who will agree with you, who will be upset by what you say, and who will be angry or offended."

These seasoned women preachers validated the reality of awareness of and anxiety over relationship in their preaching ministry. One preacher said, "My congregation affirms my preaching." She was asked, "Does that ease your anxiety?" Her response, "No, it's more than ever. I don't relax a bit until I see them giving signals three to four minutes into the sermon of receiving it positively."

The women preachers asserted that the size of the congregation, small or large, made no difference in their level of anxiety.

A senior woman pastor was quite candid about her experience: "At some point I decided I did not want to be controlled by other people's expectations and I started stating clearly my views on issues. Boy, did I make people mad at me."

Interviews and comments make clear that women bring psychological issues to the preaching ministry. It is pertinent to explore further the roots of these internal dynamics and issues. One of these issues was named by a student: "Women seem to struggle more with the issue of authenticity in preaching. For me, the question is how to be a real person in preaching." Another student added, "One thing is to work with the text. I need to be living with it [the text]. I ask myself, 'What is God saying to me?'"

Another issue evident in interviews with women preachers is summarized in this question posed by a woman seminarian: "How do I stay connected to people and speak the truth?" Discussions with women preachers seem to reveal three themes that are central to their internal dynamics and responses to preaching. They are:

Authenticity before God

❖ Faithfulness in hearing and speaking what God reveals in Scripture, church history, and tradition.

Authenticity of self

❖ Authenticity in speaking truthfully about reality as the woman preacher experiences it.

Authenticity in community

❖ To preach in a way that builds a strong relationship with others—the hearer, the congregation, the church.

❖ To preach in a way that does not provoke alienation or rejection.

In reviewing the data and narrative material from women preachers, the pertinence of other current research on the psychological development of women and girls seems evident. Current research documents women's struggles to develop and maintain authentic voice. Inquiries into the issues and dynamics described by women preachers attest to their struggle for authentic voice.

Educational theory illuminates this struggle. Educators have long stressed the value of role models in education. I have found role models to be a wonderful resource in educating women about voice retrieval and in the teaching of preaching. Positive role models help women overcome internal tension and ambivalence due to the risks inherent in voice use and preaching.

As I developed as a preacher, I kept seeking other women preachers as role models from whom to learn style and technique. Later, as a seminary professor, I developed a course in preaching entitled "Models and Techniques of Preaching." It was structured to encourage women students to interview and listen to other women preachers as a way of educating themselves as preachers. In the course I lamented the lack of women preachers in the church's history. The women students went on a hunt to find women preachers in various historical periods. They brought in the writings of Julian of Norwich, Hildegard of Bingen, Sojourner Truth, abbesses, saints, and so on. They said, "Here is the preaching of women in history." I realized that we had defined preaching as what happens in a pulpit—a narrow definition I had learned but did not really accept.

The students were right. I began to seek the voice of women in the church and equate it with preaching. I recalled sewing circles, quilting bees, church suppers, bazaars. Were those the pulpits—the preaching arena—for women? I heard the voices of women proclaiming the gospel to others, relating it to their lives and history. There was the dialogue of gospel and reality in the company of the people of God.

Preaching

No question about it. How had I, or for that matter we as women, not heard and recognized women's preaching? Why had the church not heard their preaching? Because our ears were closed. The listener could not hear the voices of women preaching. Women did not understand themselves to be preaching, either. I suggest that both factors combine to create a serious block to women's voices in the church in the past and in the present.

As we come to understand these barriers we will be able to retrieve women's voices in the past and empower them in the present. We must challenge the church to address its resistance to women's voices.

But, perhaps by now, the reader is feeling some resistance to these views. Resistance to women's voices is so inherent in our society and the church, we can assume that such resistance resides in all of us to some degree.

The issue is how one responds to that resistance whether woman preacher, congregation member, church leader, or seminary professor.

The material I have presented thus far is very provocative. An article on the preaching ministry of women in the Yale Divinity School publication, *Reflections,* was vehemently attacked by a local church leader. He totally rejected the notion of a distinctiveness in women's preaching and the concept of women seeking "authentic voice" in the relationship of self to God and others.

Other critics have questioned the emphasis on person and authentic voice as leading to a subjective, overly personal approach to preaching, which, in turn, might lead to a dangerous relativism in preaching.

I address these critiques by relating the issue of authenticity in preaching to some theological approaches relevant in preaching.

Preaching is God drawing us, preacher and hearer, into the event of Christ among us as the Word of God. It is the engagement of preacher and hearer with the Word of God. It is the engagement of preacher and hearer with scripture, with each other, and with the reality of the world. In this engagement of mind and soul, self and other, God speaks.

It is not the preacher's word or the sermon alone that provides this engagement but the total event of scripture, sermon preparation, preacher preparation, sermon delivery, and hearer's receiving of and interaction with the read scripture, spoken word, heard word, and personal dialogue and reflection with the Christian community. Preaching must be "in the midst" of the gathered people of God, the congregation. It is an event that takes place on an individual and corporate or community level. The preacher is in dialogue with God, scripture, church teaching, congregation, and world. So is the hearer. In this dialogue, this engagement, God's Word is

heard, and the work of the preacher and the hearer is to
hear God's Word and to carry that Word into the world.
God does this work in our midst—through all of it and
through everyone.

Within the church, women's voices have not been
attended to or "heard." Women's voices are difficult for
the hearer to "hear." Years ago, I was invited to preach
at the ordination of a friend. This was in the early days
of women priests in the Episcopal Church, so we were
still an unpredictable oddity to many people, especially
to other priests. I arrived very early for the service for I
like to gain some familiarity with the layout and the
acoustics of the church. The rector, the priest in charge
of the parish, greeted me and gave me a tour of the
church. When we arrived at the pulpit, he looked anx-
iously at me and said, "We have an amplification sys-
tem. You see the microphone here. But you must speak
directly and loudly into the microphone because otherwise you will never be heard." I responded that I was
familiar with microphones and that I had a very fully
developed vocal capacity since I had been active in
drama in college.

He looked unconvinced and said more firmly that it
was very important that I speak loudly and directly into
the microphone. He recounted stories of preachers who
had failed to do so and what a failure their sermons had
been. A few minutes later, he came bustling forward and
said they were ready to test the microphone. I went to
the pulpit and spoke several sentences into the microphone. He came rushing forward and said, "Why that
was just fine, try it again." He sounded as if he couldn't
believe there wasn't a problem hearing me. I spoke into
the microphone again. "Could you hear her, Sid?" he
shouted to the balcony. "Great," said Sid in the shadow
of the balcony. In relief, he turned to me and said, "I
think you'll do just fine." I had been fairly sure I would

do "just fine." I knew I had a capable, trained voice and
was determined to be heard. Once again, it was presumed a woman could not be heard. Once again, it was
surprising when the woman could be heard.

The church has not sought to listen to or welcome
the voices of women. Women have not been placed in
the designated role of preacher in the church. The
church assumed, and so did most women, that men's
voices spoke for women. The church assumed that the
voices of men and women were the same. Much is the
same, but much differs. It is essential to hear the many
voices of the people of God. Women need to find ways to
listen better to their voices, maintain their voices in dialogue with others' voices, and retrieve their voices. Congregations need to seek out and welcome women's
voices as preachers, as teachers, as leaders. For the
preacher, woman or man, this is not an unfocused or
undisciplined process. Indeed not; rather, it is an effort
of the spirit and the soul. The preacher and the hearer
need to attend to the soul, attend to the life of the Spirit
personally through prayer, Bible study, worship, meditation, discussion, mission, and teaching. The church
names and illuminates these resources.

The preacher must come to the preaching task seeking not only to be the good scholar, researcher, or student. These are the roles most familiar to us as a result
of educational experiences in school and seminary. Yes,
one may draw on these approaches, but a preacher
should not stop there. Christian spiritual discipline nur-
tures the soul through study, meditation, work, community, worship, and prayer. Thus, preacher and hearer
come as hungry souls seeking God's Word. That hunger
helps prepare each to engage with God's Word. That
hunger for God's Word motivates both preacher and
hearer to attend to God's voice within themselves and
within the preaching event.

What follows is a brief exploration of some theological themes which inform my understanding of how preaching and theology relate to each other.

Imago Dei is a Latin term meaning "image of God." This christological theme is found in the New Testament and in the early Christian tradition. Human persons are created according to the image of God. Through sin, the image of God is distorted in us. Through Christ, the image of God is revealed and realized. Christ restores the image of God in us so that we can move toward God and God's purpose for us. We are called to live as those reclaiming Christ in ourselves and others. For preaching, this dynamic process means preacher and hearer reclaim Christ in each other.

Another theological theme which informs the preacher's work is that of God's creative Word. In Genesis we learn that God's Word creates the world and all that is in it. The Gospel of John tells us that God's Word became flesh in Christ, creating a new order, a new reality, a new world. The preacher shares in God's creative work in discerning and proclaiming the Word of God. Through God's continuing creative work in the world, the preaching event is made part of God's revelation, part of the encounter of humanity with God. God's creative work is not a one-time event, but is a continuing reality, and it embraces the preaching event. Preacher and hearer participate together, sharing in God's creative work.

A final perspective, and the most compelling one for me, is that of liberation theology. It speaks of the liberating Word of God. We as preacher and hearer participate in God's liberating Word. We see it at work in Christ's ministry, where the sinful divisions in the present world are overcome and the voices of the people of God are liberated.

In the preaching event, preacher and hearer are called

to be liberated by God's grace through attending to each other's voice. The preacher seeks to be liberated, to be his or her fullest, freest self, and to embrace the voices of others. In radically inclusive dialogue with one another, God is at work liberating each person individually and the church corporately. To exclude oneself from full participation and leadership in the church, as many women have, is to withhold from the church the fullest possible understanding of God's Word, God's revelation, and God's work in the world. For the church to exclude women or any other category of persons from full participation and leadership in the church is to limit the work of God, and to set up barriers to the promised new order of heaven and earth in the resurrected Christ.[1]

Within these theological views, preacher and hearer would be urged to be more attentive to God's presence in self and other. Each would trust in God's embrace of her or his humanity and seek to love self and other as God does. Such theological perspectives undergird my urging that the preacher attend to her or his inner voice. That voice is loved by God; it is precious to God. Her voice must be seen as precious to God and as precious to the church. The woman preacher is loved by God and made in God's image: body, heart, mind, soul, *and* voice.

It is important to assert that in addition to the personal dimension of voice retrieval, there is a very significant corporate dimension, that is, the vision of and structure of the church. In discussing voice retrieval with Byron Stuhlman, a scholar who has written extensively in the area of liturgics and pastoral theology, he articulated this challenge well:

> Retrieving women's voices involves more than ordaining women, giving them access to the same roles in worship that men have, and giving them equal places with men in the governance of the church. It really involves a different

vision of the relationship of Christians within the church
—a different ecclesiology. It involves restructuring society.
And that brings with it both struggle and pain.[2]

To be faithful, for the woman preacher, is to trust God
to be at work in her voice, in her sermon. Her effort to
preach is loved by God. Preacher and hearer cling to the
belief that in their human encounter in the preaching
event, God is revealed. This belief enables the preacher
to take the terrifying risk of preaching—a task that is so
self-revealing that it is one of the ministry's greatest
challenges. Hear the words of Isaiah as he confronted his
fear of speaking in the Lord's name:

> In the year that King Uzziah died, I saw the Lord sitting
> on a throne, high and lofty; and the hem of his robe filled
> the temple. Seraphs were in attendance above him; each
> had six wings: with two they covered their faces, and
> with two they covered their feet, and with two they flew.
> And one called to another and said:
> "Holy, holy, holy is the LORD of hosts;
>   the whole earth is full of his glory."
> The pivots on the thresholds shook at the voices of those
> who called, and the house filled with smoke. And I said:
> "Woe is me! I am lost, for I am a man of unclean lips, and
> I live among a people of unclean lips; yet my eyes have
> seen the King, the LORD of hosts!"
>   Then one of the seraphs flew to me, holding a live coal
> that had been taken from the altar with a pair of tongs.
> The seraph touched my mouth with it and said: "Now
> that this has touched your lips, your guilt has departed
> and your sin is blotted out." Then I heard the voice of the
> Lord saying, "Whom shall I send, and who will go for
> us?" And I said, "Here am I; send me!" (Isa. 6:1-8)

The confidence of the preacher is based in God's love
of her humanity and God's use of that humanity to bring

fruit in the preaching task. Of course, the pitfall here is that confidence in God's love and working can be misappropriated by preacher and hearer to allow each to become inattentive, undisciplined, and irresponsible. Another pitfall is for the preacher to hide from the risk of exposing her or his humanity by preaching in conformity to social norms, "safe preaching." At various times in the church's history, preaching has resembled a lecture, a pastoral discourse, a diatribe, a meditation, a conversation. There have been fashions in preaching, and the preacher must resist the temptation to submerge her or his humanity in the currently acceptable preaching style.

I urge women to attend to their inner voices, and I suggest resources for doing so. This attention to the inner voice of self, which I call the retrieval of a woman's voice, is essential at this time in the church's history because women preachers face so many challenges to their voices. A concerted effort to retrieve voice is vital to women and to the church. That conviction and that work—the retrieval of women's voices— hold great promise for preaching and for the church.

CHAPTER 3

Voice Formation in Women Preachers

When I was a child I sang in the choir. I had a very low voice and would have sung a tenor part, but I decided that I didn't want to sing that part and be with all the guys. So, I decided not to sing in my actual voice range but forced my voice to sing in the alto section.

This group has pressed me to let my voice relax and let it be deep and natural. It has been an important improvement in my preaching. After these months, it dawned on me that I was still singing in the alto section of the choir. I decided to change sections and sing in the tenor section where my voice belongs and is comfortable. It was interesting because the choir director didn't want me to change. I became aware of how symbolic this was. As an adolescent, I consciously refused to accept my voice. This spring, I have consciously chosen to use my real voice—as a preacher and as a singer.

—A woman seminarian

HARVARD UNIVERSITY AND THE STONE CENTER AT Wellesley College are collaborating on research on the psychological development of women and girls. Psychologist Carol Gilligan is a central figure in the research effort. The research on voice formation in girls has implications for the preaching and leadership of women in the church. In this chapter we examine some of the research and the related issues for women in the church.

Early in her career Gilligan studied women's moral development. Her book *In a Different Voice* recorded her observations of women's moral decision making. She revealed that men and women differ in the decision-making process. She noted that women seem to empha-size the impact of their moral decisions on others. Men seem to focus more on ethical principles and moral dic-tates. Women also reflect on the impact their actions might have on specific individuals. Women ponder what impact an action might have on a significant other—a son, a daughter, a spouse, a parent, or a friend.

Gilligan pursued this inquiry by studying the moral decision making of adolescent girls. Gilligan is one of a number of researchers to become intrigued with women's responsiveness to others, or what is now termed *relationality.* In her article "Exit—Voice Dilemmas in Adolescent Development" from *Mapping the Moral Domain,* Gilligan notes that for girls, "see-ing and knowing" can threaten relationships. "Not see-ing," "not knowing," and "not voicing" are evident in the behavior of girls as a means of preserving relation-ships.

Gilligan's data indicate that adolescent girls focus on relationships more than adolescent boys do and that relationality is a priority in girls' moral decision making. Gilligan observed girls changing their behavior in order to preserve relationships, thus demonstrating the impor-tance of relationality in girls.

In a 1991 address entitled "Joining the Resistance,"[1] Carol Gilligan made clear that not only are girls very conscious of the impact of various behaviors on rela-tionships, but that adolescent girls alter their behavior

to preserve relationships. Gilligan and her team
observed that when girls perceive relationships to be
threatened, their perceptions of reality may alter or
become blocked due to fears of disrupting relationships.

In 1993 at a conference sponsored by Harvard Medical
School, Carol Gilligan reported on her current project,
which involves extensive study and observation of and
interviews with adolescent girls. The girls keep journals
in which they discuss the events and relationships of
their lives. The girls speculate about the interactions of
men and women, their responses to each other, and the
responses of adults to the adolescent girls. The girls are
also observed scanning faces of friends and adults, particularly as they take sharp notice of who wants to be
with them. Their journal assignments require them to
comment on poetry, literature, paintings, and sculpture.
For example, in studying paintings the girls write imag-
ined male-female conversations.

Gilligan postulates that what the girls choose not to see
and thus "not know" distorts the girls' perceptions of both
self and reality. Gilligan believes this becomes a major
problem for girls in adolescence, especially when a girl rec-
ognizes differences between her perceptions and other
commonly held points of view. Gilligan quotes Anna, an
adolescent in the study, as saying, "Why can't you see this
the way I do? Why do you make me feel there's something
wrong with me?" Anna feels she has to hold in her feelings, her views, to stay in relationship.[2] Gilligan dubs this
process "loss of voice." The girls appear to ponder what
voices people like to listen to, or "hear" from girls, so they
can adjust their own voices accordingly. The research sug-
gests that girls adjust their voices to avoid being labeled
"mad" or "bad" or "stupid" by peers and valued adults.
These three designations—"mad," "bad," and "stupid"—
appear repeatedly in girls' journals and are attributed to
women in paintings and sculptures.

Researchers report girls "taking note of the emotional climate, noticing who wants to be with whom, noticing who is angry, noticing who has overstepped a line, who has hurt another."[3]

When the girls interpret the reality that is presented to them in art or literature, they fantasize and project onto male and female figures. Comments like, "This is how he felt," "This is how she felt," "This is what she said," and "This is what he said," are found often in the girls' journals.[4]

The Harvard/Stone Center research shows that at adolescence, there is an increase in girls' desire for relationship. Girls reveal that they study male and female adults in relationship. The girls constantly impute emotions and attachments between persons. There seems to be a self-defined code within each girl as to what can be noted, what must be ignored, what can be spoken, and what cannot be spoken. A constant "watchfulness" develops. Girls' relationships to others cause them great concern within their social groupings. The subjects of "who is friends with whom" and "who is angry with whom" are constantly discussed with others and in journals. When this research is presented at conferences, adult women indicate that their adolescent experiences confirm these findings.

Such thinking in girls fosters a disconnection between self and reality. Hungering for relationship, the young girl idealizes others, endowing them with wisdom, insight, affirmation, and recognition. Thoughts of "she knows everything," "she's always right," and "she's so together" permeate the girls' journals.[5] Negative feelings about self such as, "She doesn't like me; I must be a terrible person," are evident, also. The girls' writings indicate vulnerability of self. The recurrent idealization of self and idealization of others, and disappointment in self or disappointment in others, point to the vulnerability of self-concept.

Researchers have studied the impact of mothers and adult women on adolescent girls to see how they affect loss of voice. The following observation is indicative of the findings:

A mother and a daughter go shopping for a dress. The mother shows her daughter a dress she has picked out and asks, "How do you like this dress?" The daughter says, "I don't like it." The mother becomes angry and impatient. The daughter says, "Why do you ask me when you don't want to hear my opinion, because you yell at me when I tell you?"[6]

Researchers worked with female teachers grading the schoolwork of adolescent girls. The girls were assigned the task of critiquing a poem about an older man who praises the beauty and sensuality of a young girl. One girl labeled the poem "terrible," condemning it as "indecent and frightening." The teacher gave the paper a low grade, stating the girl had misunderstood the theme of the poem. The teacher told the girl that the poem is about sexual fantasies between men and women. The teacher criticized the girl: "You did not critique the poem. Your personal reaction to the poem is not relevant."[7] This is an example of a woman saying to a young girl, "Your perception of reality is neither valid nor valued. You see and hear in this poem something that is not there." This teacher's response to the views and the voice of an adolescent girl is an example of how adult women can contribute to the suppression of voice in girls.

Such instances were prevalent in the Harvard/Stone Center research with teacher-student and mother-daughter relationships. When an adolescent girl's schoolwork did not conform to the norm, that is, the traditional interpretation of a literary work or a work of art, the young girl received a lower grade. Adult women were often observed aligning themselves with the forces that resist and reject voice in the young girls. The young girls identified with the women and had a powerful desire to maintain positive relationships with them.

Relationality, the desire to be in relationship, pressed the young girl to conform to the values and perspectives of her peers and esteemed adults. The young girl, who had been tentatively testing her voice, began to experience vulnerability and ambivalence about using her voice. Research revealed the systematic discounting of the young girl's voice and perception of reality.[8] This compounds the loss of voice in girls and women.

Currently, researchers are examining how young girls ascertain what is safe to be seen and described. They are studying how girls weigh what is seen, what is heard, and what is known versus what is safe to express to peers or adults. This research is being conducted with a group of girls selected to assure diversity in terms of ethnicity, race, education, class, and economic level.

Some of the research findings are fascinating. For example, at age 12, the number of "I know" statements made by a girl in an interview might number 63. By the age of 14, the number declined by two-thirds. In addition, a significant increase in the number of times girls responded, "I don't know," was noted. One researcher cited a case in which "I don't know" was said in response to questions 21 times during the course of an interview with a 12-year-old girl. At age 13, "I don't know" was said 67 times as a response by the same girl, and at age 14, 135 times.[9] There was a significant increase in the "I don't know" statements in most interviews. The interviews were punctuated, at age 14, with "you know." By age 14, girls attributed what is "known" to the interviewer, a teacher, a friend, with the phrase "you know."

When a young girl says, "I don't know" or "you know," is she acknowledging loss of voice? The shifting responses coupled with observations seem to confirm that the girl is abdicating her voice. She seems to be refusing to say what she knows, probably due to loss of confidence about self, reality, and relationship security. It is difficult to ascertain if she is refusing to say what she knows or if she doesn't know that she knows it. The young girl seems to go through a process of some conscious and unconscious suppression of her voice. Research indicates a deep level of psychological detachment, dissociation, and confusion are present.

Recently, Carol Gilligan has focused on a process designed to help parents and teachers work to retain the voices of adolescent girls. It is Gilligan's theory, drawn from her research, that the girl who is seen as nonconforming and troublesome, who talks too much, who says things that hurt people's feelings, who is an outspoken leader in her group, who talks back, or who doesn't listen to her parents is actually the girl who resists this process of losing her voice. In her defiance, such a girl fights to retain her voice. She is the girl who is most likely to move through adolescence and attain the greatest individuation and autonomy as an adult woman.[10] So, the young girl who is more rejecting of social norms seems to reach the end of adolescence with a more intact sense of self. These girls seem to develop greater autonomy than those who conform to society's ideals. The threat the young girl faces in this struggle is the loss of relationality, or relationship to her peers and to adults. The issue for girls and women is how to have self-determination and maintain relationality. It is a crucial dilemma for girls and women. It is a crucial dilemma for women preachers and women leaders in the church.

A concept that helps clarify this dilemma is that of agency described in the work of psychiatrist Jean Baker Miller in her theories on the psychological development of women.[11] If the development of agency, or self-deter-

mination, threatens relationships, then it is a very difficult dilemma for girls and women. The dilemma, as a
woman moves through adolescence and into adulthood,
is how to have self-determination or agency and maintain relationality. Janet L. Surrey, Ph.D., in her work
with the Stone Center has written extensively on the
"self-in-relation" theory.[12]

It is very clear that girls and women monitor voice
and behavior to varying degrees so as to preserve relationality. Books like *Meeting at the Crossroads, Women,
Girls and Psychotherapy, Women in Travail and Transition, Mother Daughter Revolution,* and *Women's
Growth in Connection* review the research and issues I
have referred to in this chapter. The research I have summarized is prompting discussion and acclaim within the
psychological community. This response demonstrates
the importance of concepts like relationality and loss of
voice.

Implications for Women Preachers

I have spent the past two years discussing these concepts with students and faculty of various seminaries,
with many women clergy, and with numerous congregations. In each arena, the results have been the same.
A very large percentage of women find the research illuminates their experiences as adolescents and adults.
Women preachers particularly appreciate the concepts
and data. Many find the research helps them identify
and understand processes that they experienced but
hadn't understood. Again and again, women preachers
have stated that these concepts have helped them
understand the particular issues with which they as
preachers wrestle: relationality, voice and agency. Perhaps most important, the research helps women
preachers realize that the issues are generated not by

their individual psychological makeup but by the common psychological developmental history of women. As one woman put it:

> We've named the problem, but it's not mine alone. I'm not the problem. Rather, the problem is generated outside me and shared by lots of women. So, I'm not weak or neurotic or anxiety-ridden which is what I thought might be the case. We named the issue. It exists in me. It's generated by forces inside and outside me. It's a problem for me, for congregations, for the church, and for the culture. Instead of feeling I'm inadequate, I can now focus on the task of how to respond to the problem. I am working now on what I can do to preach with less tension and greater effectiveness. These research findings have freed me and energized me.

My theory is that preaching, more than any other form of public address or communication, is one in which a woman feels called to express what she knows. Yet, in the very process of preaching—of "giving voice" to what she sees and knows—a woman risks her relationship to God, her relationship to self, and her relationship to others. What choices does a woman face? To betray her relationship to God by not testifying to what she knows? To devalue herself and her voice? Women preachers tell me, "I have to say this because this is the truth as I know it, but I feel the tension. I wonder, 'What is the Word of God here?' Do I dare speak it?" My interviews with women preachers document feelings of great tension regarding voice. "Do I dare say what I believe?" they ask.

Within the field of homiletics, men and women are warned against being overly personal in preaching. Students are cautioned not to presume to speak from a personal perspective. That admonition further suppresses voices that have rarely dared to speak. It is dangerous advice to those whose voices have been excluded in the church—women, persons of color, and disadvantaged persons. If the church is to experience the rich insights of these long-stifled voices, there must be a new attentiveness to and encouragement of these voices on the part of those who teach preaching.

Yes, women preachers can come to understand the internal tensions inherent for them in the preaching task. Yet many educators assume that women "have difficulty preaching and being heard," as one homiletics professor flatly declared. The task is rather that churches and seminaries should seek to elicit women's voices—not only for the sake of women but for the sake of the church!

My development as a preacher and my work in the teaching of preaching have convinced me of the importance of voice development and the complexity of the response to women's voices in the church.

As I developed as a preacher, regular experience of other women preachers was a very positive influence. Later, as a professor teaching preaching, I developed courses incorporating such role models educationally. As I mentioned in chapter 2 as an assignment, I asked women students to interview and observe women preachers. They sought the voices of women in the church's history, also. They brought in the writings of various women saints. They said, "Here is the preaching of women in history." The students were right. Throughout history, women found vehicles for proclaiming the Word of God. Together we listened to the voices of women proclaiming the gospel, relating it to their lives and their world. It was the dialogue of gospel and reality. It was women preaching! But we did not hear women's voices. We resisted women's voices. Women did not understand themselves to *be* preaching. Both factors created a block to women's voices in the church in the past, and the obstacles continue today.

I choose to label this nonrecognition "cultural resistance to women's voices." As we come to understand this cultural resistance, we will be able to retrieve women's voices in the past and empower women's voices in the present. The church must address its resistance to women's voices. How can the church recognize, encourage, and "hear" women's voices? It is a formidable task, but it is under way. Women's voices have been lost through inattention, devaluation, threat, and cultural resistance. Can the voices be retrieved? Absolutely.

CHAPTER 4

Faithfulness, Agency, and Voice Retrieval

re-trieve 1. *to recover or regain.* 2. *to bring back to a former and better state; restore.* 3. *to make amends for; make good repair: to retrieve an error.* 4. *to recall to mind.* 5. *(of hunting dogs) to fetch (killed or wounded game).* 6. *to draw back or reel in (a fishing line).* 7. *to rescue or save (as in tennis, handball, etc.) to make an in-bounds return of (a difficult shot).* 8. *to locate and read (data) from computer storage, as the display on the monitor.* 9. *to retrieve game.* 10. *to retrieve a fishing line.* 11. *the act of retrieving, recovery.*

—*Random House Dictionary of the English Language*

GIVEN A NEW PERSPECTIVE ON THE ISSUE OF VOICE IN PREACHING, a woman preacher can consciously work to retrieve and strengthen her voice—a process I have called "retrieval of voice." Voice retrieval is essential to more effective preaching. This chapter discusses voice retrieval and the relevant concepts of faithfulness, agency, and power. A format for voice retrieval that has been designed and used with women is presented here.

Faithfulness and Voice Retrieval

"What does it mean to be a faithful woman?" Faithful women are engaged in hearing their own and others'

voices. Being faithful means using one's voice in a dialogue with God, with others, with the world, and with
the church. To be a faithful woman is to be engaged in a
retrieval of women's voices in the past and the present.
As discussed in chapter 2 this retrieval of women's
voices requires a multidisciplinary effort drawing on the
resources of developmental psychology, behavioral psychology, history, and spirituality.

Retrieving women's voices means consistently living in
the realization that God gives us gifts, resources, voices,
and power. It means being suspicious of self-denial. A
faithful woman does not inhibit her voice, as we were
taught. Faithful women risk believing that God does not
want us to mute our voices. Faithful women struggle to
find and to use our voices. We listen to each other's voice.
We are called to honor each other's voice, not avoiding
conflict or anger but hearing and accepting differences. It
is in the facing of the differences and the experience of not
losing relationships that we begin to trust that our voices
will not cost us Christian community. In facing differences and retaining community, women are affirmed and
empowered. The Christian community involved in welcoming women's voices is confirming God's acceptance
and affirmation of women. This is the role of the congregation in the work of retrieving women's voices, and it is
a vital role.

The Stone Center research on power and agency in
women's lives is pertinent to the work of voice retrieval.
Agency is defined as the ability to be an agent for oneself
in contact with others and with one's environment. In
*Women's Growth in Connection: Writings from the
Stone Center*, Dr. Jean Baker Miller, a psychiatrist who
is acclaimed for her writings on the psychological development of women, states that women seek empowerment through relationships and through their work with

others in group settings. Empowerment is acceptable for women when they use power with and for others. Miller proposes understanding power to be the capacity to "move or produce change" and that this new understanding of power should replace the idea of power as dominion, control, or mastery.[1]

Miller's redefinition of power would seem congruent with the way women exercise power in the church. In the church, women characteristically acquire power in conjunction with others. Study of the lives of women in the church seems to reveal that women use their personal and institutional power for the benefit of others. The lives of women saints, as we examine them, attest to themes of agency and advocacy.

As we seek to understand voice retrieval, we do well to survey the lives of faithful women who exercised leadership in the church in the past. History seems to confirm the themes that emerge in the research on women's psychological development and voice development. The issues of voice and agency are evident in the biographies and writings of many saints. I chose to study four women saints and their writings: Julian of Norwich, Teresa of Avila, Hildegard of Bingen, and Catherine of Siena. What follows is a brief summary of their lives and writings with emphasis on their use of voice and the response of family, society, and church to their voices. I am aware that my examples represent four European women from the Middle Ages whose stories have survived in the European church. One yearns for the stories and voices of other cultural and ethnic groups. I am grateful that other groundbreaking work along these lines is being done by Teresa Fry, a professor of homiletics at Emory, who is studying spirituals, diaries, sermons, and other primary source material to retrieve the voice of African American women.

Julian of Norwich
1342–1416

Julian was a holy woman, an anchoress, a special vocation conferred by the church in which one lived in solitude in a cell attached to a church. She spent all her time in contemplation, prayer, and the spiritual counsel of others. Upon entering her cell, an anchoress never left it, remaining in residence there until death. Julian lived in fourteenth-century England in the era of the Black Death, the plague that devastated much of Europe and Asia. She carried on her work of prayer, contemplation, spiritual counsel, and writing in a large city, Norwich, which was a center of business, culture, and ecclesiastical vigor. Julian lived with the threats of the plague, heresy charges, and the political currents of church and state. Certainly, she faced many risks in giving voice to her visions and teachings on God's love. Several colleagues cautioned her to be careful what she wrote lest she be convicted of heresy. Yet, she used her voice, and her writings are a treasure for Christians. Thomas Merton, in his book *Seeds of Destruction*, wrote,

> Julian is, without doubt, one of the most wonderful of all Christian voices. She gets greater and greater in my eyes as I grow older, and whereas in the old days I used to be crazy about St. John of the Cross, I would not exchange him now for Julian if you gave me the world and the Indies and all the Spanish mystics rolled up in one bundle. I think that Julian of Norwich is, with Newman, the greatest English theologian.[2]

Julian authored one of the first books in Middle English, and she rivals Chaucer for the honor of writing the first book in England. Julian's book, *Revelations of Divine Love*, is the first English-language book written by a woman. *Revelations of Divine Love* is an eloquent, vibrant account of a series of visions that revealed to Julian the profound nature of God's love. Julian records in her first pages the ambivalence she felt about writing: "Because I am a woman, ought I therefore to believe that I should not tell you the goodness of God, although I saw at that time that it is His will that it be known."[3] Introducing his acclaimed book, *A Lesson of Love,* Father John Julian praises the clarity and accessibility of Julian's voice,

> A contemporary of Chaucer, Julian of Norwich wrote this book in Middle English at a time when the language was still in its infancy; her spelling, grammar and sentence construction reflect this formative time in the development of English. As a result, although her ideas are wonderfully clear and simple, and intended for all her fellow Christians, access to her work has been limited by linguistic problems. There have been four translations of *The Revelations of Divine Love* in the past fifteen years, but these have often been marked by too academic, too literal or too paraphrased a translation. . . . There is present in her work a . . . clarity of image that is nothing short of profound.[4]

Listen to Julian's eloquent voice in these words from her revelation:

> Also in this revelation He showed a little thing, the size of an hazel nut in the palm of my hand, and it was as round as a ball. I looked at it with the eye of my understanding and thought: "What can this be?" And it was generally answered thus: "It is all that is made." I marveled how it could continue, because it seemed to me it could suddenly have sunk into nothingness because of its littleness. And I was answered in my understanding: "It continueth and always shall, because God loveth it; and in this way *everything* hath its being by the love of God." In this little thing I saw three characteristics:

the first is that God made it,
the second is that God loves it,
the third, that God keeps it.
But what did I observe in that?
Truly the Maker, the Lover, and the Keeper for, until I
am in essence one-ed to Him, I can never have full rest
nor true joy.[5]

Julian's writings were copied and cherished throughout the church in England, though not by church authorities. Many persons sought her spiritual counsel. She
spoke out on political and social issues and was very
influential in Norwich.

Julian experienced threat to her voice. She must have
feared that charges of heresy would be brought against
her, the consequence of which would have been death at
the stake. Church authorities scrutinized Julian's teaching and writings. To author a book as she did was a great
risk; for in disclosing one's spiritual teachings, one
encountered the church's examination and potential
condemnation. Julian faced this risk, yet spoke and
wrote brilliantly of God's love. Her work reveals spiritual knowledge and theological understanding of great
depth.

Teresa of Avila
1515–82

St. Teresa was born Therese de Cepeda y Ahumada in
Castile, Spain, in 1515. Jesus Castellano, a Vatican
authority on St. Teresa's life and teaching, has written of
her:

St. Teresa of Jesus constitutes a cultural phenomenon
of widespread impact: (1) by reason of her person, her
doctrine, and her literary style which have had and continue to have *wide impact in the Church and in society;*

(2) because she was a woman who carried out a spiritual mission in the Church of her time and who left, unique among early writers and theologians, a theological and spiritual doctrine that grows out of her own Christian experience and bears the *seal of her Christian feminism*; and (3) for the openness of social and human values found in her writings and joined to her deep Christian, evangelical experience which embraces the summits of the *Christian mystical life.*[6]

Teresa was one of twelve children. She had no formal education as a child, but her family encouraged her to learn to read with her brothers. She lived in Avila in the sixteenth century.

Biographers note that Teresa was considered a rebellious young girl. When she was an adolescent, her father sent her to a convent in an attempt to keep her safe and under control. Illness forced her to return home after several years at the convent.

At the age of twenty-one, Teresa decided to enter the Carmelite order. Convent life was not a harsh one. It involved social contact with men and women, fine food, and dancing. There was little emphasis on prayer or worship.

After meditating on the passion of Christ and experiencing a vision, Teresa felt called to reform the Carmelites through founding a new convent community. She received permission to do this and thus began the reformed order, the Discalced Carmelites. She abolished distinctions between women of nobility and peasant women within the convent. Everyone had to cook and clean. Small cells replaced sitting rooms. The day held long hours of prayer.

Teresa's reforms and egalitarian views earned her the love and respect of the faithful people of Spain. She traveled extensively, founding and visiting convents, encoun-

tering theologians, church leaders, and political leaders.
All came to value her spiritual and secular guidance.

> In Spain's golden age . . . she found herself involved in
> the most varied affairs: differences between the king and
> the family of the Duke of Alba; threats of war between
> Spain and Portugal; litigations in her own family; clashes
> between the Castilian and Andalusian temperament, and
> between conflicting commands from the royal govern-
> ment and Rome.[7]

Teresa began writing at the insistence of her confessor
who held spiritual authority over her in the order. She
completed her first book, *A Life,* in 1565 and expressed
therein great ambivalence in giving voice to her spiritual
knowledge. "For a long time, even though God favored
me, I didn't know what words to use to explain His favors,
and this was no small trial."[8] But God did empower and
equip Teresa to speak as she states again in *A Life.* "The
difficulty was that I didn't know how to say either little
or much about my prayer, for only recently did God give
me this favor of understanding what it is and knowing
how to speak about it."[9] Speak she does, and with startling eloquence: "This prayer, then, is a little spark of the
Lord's true love which he begins to enkindle in the soul;
and he desires that the soul grow in the understanding of
what this love accompanied by delight is. For anyone who
has experience, it is impossible not to understand soon
that this little spark cannot be acquired."[10]

Teresa went on to write six books, some poetry, and
extensive correspondence.

In addition to internal, personal tension regarding
voice, Teresa experienced anxiety and fear over how her
voice would be received. Church authorities reviewed
her first book, and she was forced to change parts of it.
Members of the Inquisition in Spain examined all of her

works. Condemnation by the Inquisition could have led to censure and death. She lived with this threat as a woman giving voice to her knowledge of God.

It is possible that Teresa altered her voice so it would be understandable for persons of all classes and educational levels.[11] Other scholars think that Teresa adapted her writing style to sidestep the Inquisition.

> Teresian scholars and commentators customarily fault the saint's writing for being diffuse, rambling and lacking coherence. . . . But within the past fifteen years a new generation of scholars has subjected this stereotype to critical scrutiny by studying the rhetorical strategy of Teresa's prose works and has demonstrated that, far from being artless, Teresa is a masterful rhetorician and pragmatic stylist who carefully tunes her style to her audience.[12]

The prominence of this current perspective among scholars was confirmed by my own research at the University of Madrid in 1993, in a conversation with Maria Asuz, Ph.D., a professor of linguistics who has taught at Bryn Mawr College in the U.S. and at the University of Madrid.

Teresa died in 1582 at age sixty-seven. She was beatified on April 24, 1614, and canonized a saint on March 12, 1622. The rapidity of this recognition attests to her great influence on the church—a remarkable occurrence for a woman.

On September 27, 1970, Teresa of Avila was declared the first woman Doctor of the Church by Pope Paul VI.

Hildegard of Bingen
1098–1179

Hildegard von Bingen was born in 1098 in Bockelheim, Germany. In the recently published translation of

Hildegard's book, *Scivias,* Adelgundis Fuhrkotter has written a brief foreword that summarizes the events of Hildegard's life.

As a child, Hildegard was cared for by a learned woman who supervised her education. At maturity, she joined the Benedictine order and entered the convent. In 1136, she was elected abbess of the community. In 1141, Hildegard began work on her first book, *Scivias* ("Wisse die Wege," or "Know the Ways"). Her still incomplete work was honored at the Trier Synod (November 30, 1147, to mid-February 1148) when the Cistercian pope Eugene III fulfilled a request made by Archbishop Henry of Mainz. Eugene III read a part of her work to persons gathered there, and it was enthusiastically received. Bernard of Clairvaux as well as the pope encouraged her to continue her work. The visionary could master her earlier uncertainty and shyness, as the church's recognition of her visions strengthened her voice. Hildegard worked on *Scivias* for ten years. She wrote other books in her lifetime, one on nature and another on medicine. She produced works in drama, music, and art.

In describing her music Hildegard said,

> Underneath all the texts, all the sacred psalms, and cantides, these watery varieties of sounds and silences, terrifying, mysterious, whirling and sometimes gestating and gentle must somehow be felt in the pulse, ebb and flow of the music that sings in me. My new song must float like a feather on the breath of God.

Her lyrics for a song to the virgin mother of God convey this energy and spirit:

> Hail, O greenest branch, you who came forth in the windy blast of the questioning of saints. When the time came that you blossomed in your branches—hail, hail was (the word) to you! for the warmth of the sun distilled

in you a flower that gave fragrance to all the spices which had been dry. And they all appeared in full verdure. Hence the heavens dropped dew upon the grass and the whole earth was made glad, because her womb brought forth wheat, and because the birds of heaven had nests in it. Then a meal was prepared for humanity, and great joy for the banqueters. Hence, O sweet Virgin, in you no joy is lacking.[13]

In addition, she traveled and preached throughout northern Europe.

In Hildegard of Bingen's writings we can hear her tension regarding her voice. The following excerpts are cited from *Scivias:*

Behold, in the forty-third year of my passing journey, when I clung to a heavenly vision with fear and trembling, I saw a very great light from which a heavenly voice spoke and said to me:

"O weak person, both ashes, and decaying of the decaying, speak and write what you see and hear. Because you are timid about speaking and simple about explaining and unskilled about writing those things not according to the mouth of a person nor according to the perception of human inventiveness nor according to the wishes of human arrangement, but according to the extent that you see and hear those things in the heavens above in the marvelousness of God, bring to light those things by way of explanation, just as even a listener, understanding the words of a teacher, explains those things according to the course of the teacher's speech— willingly, plainly, and instructive. So therefore even you, o person, speak those things not according to yourself nor according to another person, but according to the will of the one knowing, see and arrange all things in the secrets of the divinity's own mysteries."

Although I saw and heard these things, I nevertheless refused to write them because of doubt and evil opinion

and because of the diversity of other people's words, not
so much out of stubbornness, but out of humility. . . . I
was able to bring my work to completion with difficulty,
taking ten years.[14]

Catherine of Siena
1347–80

Catherine was born Catherine Benincasa in 1347 in
Siena, Italy. Her life of faith was evident early in childhood through prayer and worship. In adolescence she
moved to a solitary room within her large family home.
There she remained in solitude, spending her time in
prayer and fasting. After several years, she experienced a
mandate from God to work among the sick and poor
people of Siena.

As she entered adulthood, Catherine joined the third
order of the Dominican community, which allowed her
to live and work in a secular ministry. As she continued
nursing and caring for the poor, Catherine found herself
surrounded by a diverse community of disciples drawn
to her for her love, her integrity, and her spiritual counsel. The importance of these relationships in her voice
development is evident in biographical accounts. Indica-
tions of relationality in Catherine's life are found in this
quote from the *New Catholic Encyclopedia:*

> There gathered around her the nucleus of the group of
> friends and disciples with which her name is associated:
> men and women; priests . . . and layfolk; most of them
> her seniors, but . . . all accustomed to calling her
> "mother." The formation of this "family" led in turn to
> the beginning not later than 1370, of the great series of
> Catherine's letters. . . . At first simply vehicles for spiri-
> tual formation and encouragement, the letters soon
> began to focus on public affairs. . . . She was a woman,
> young and with no social position. She was accused of

hypocrisy and presumption. At this critical point, it was her Dominican affiliation that saved her. Summoned to Florence, to give an account of herself to the general chapter of the order . . . she satisfied the rigorous judges, and her work was given official Dominican protection. . . . The next 4 years saw Catherine's influence on public affairs at its greatest.[15]

Others in Catherine's world respected her ability to transcend difference and communicate. Catherine became an intermediary negotiating the end of the Avignon papacy. She persuaded Pope Gregory XI to return to Rome, and she continued to advise him until his death. She served as a counselor to his successor in the midst of conflict between the political powers of Florence and Rome.

Catherine was a prolific writer, although there is debate among scholars as to whether she dictated her work or personally wrote it. Some scholars assert that she never was taught to write. Many books and treatises on the nature of the life of faith and extensive correspondence with disciples and leaders of church and state are attributed to her. In her book *The Dialogue*, Catherine wrote ecstatically,

> You, eternal Father, gave us memory to hold your gifts and share your power. You gave us understanding so that seeing your goodness, we might share the wisdom of your only begotten Son. And you gave us free will to love what our understanding sees and knows of your truth, and so share the mercy of your Holy Spirit. Why did you so dignify us? With unimaginable love you looked upon your creatures within your very self and you fell in love with us so it was love that made you create us and give us being just so that we might taste your supreme eternal good.[16]

She was loved and highly esteemed in Italy as indicated by her rapid canonization by the church after her death in 1380.

Catherine of Siena was designated a Doctor of the Church in 1970, the highest honor possible for a theologian in the Roman Catholic Church. Her writings contain a marvelous blend of the mystical and the practical. Many scholars have commented on the vigor and relevance of her voice. It has been said that "she was a saint who mixed fearlessly in the world and spoke with the candor and authority of one completely committed to Christ."[17] She functioned from within a beloved Christian community, whose members acknowledged their relationship of deep affection in the title "Mother." Her life work included advocacy for others in her political and social arena, nursing the sick and caring for the poor.

Again, in this saint's life, the themes of relationality through community, advocacy, and mission are present and empower her agency and voice. Power is found within community and used for the benefit of others— in this case, Catherine's local and national community. For speaking out, she suffered criticism and even a full investigation by the Dominican hierarchy. Tension, danger, and conflict with church and state leaders mark her ministry. Her voice provoked rejection and conflict. Catherine used her voice to counsel and challenge her disciples, her community, and her church.

Women Saints and Women's Voices Today in the Church

These insights from the lives of women saints are significant and bear consideration in the work of voice retrieval. In such work, I assign each woman in class a saint to research. She is to study and report on the life and teachings of the saint. Each woman returns with a report for the group. We hear the reports and discuss the themes that emerge. The group lists the characteristics of the voice of each woman saint. The voices of women saints have been described variously as:

Loyal
Unwavering
True to herself
Just
Strong together
Assertive
Political
Educated
Defiant
Determined
Clever

The women identify with the women saints. The women see the tremendous power in the accounts of the lives of these women saints. The word *power* is rarely used to describe them. Rather, they are portrayed as humble, loving, and self-denying in many biographies. It is fascinating to ask, "What is being confirmed as holy?" We also must ask, "Who sets the criteria for sainthood? Who confers the designation *saint* on a woman?" There is much discussion of the issue of assertiveness among women saints. The group notes the dangers women saints faced in giving voice, such as charges of heresy, family rejection, poverty, rebuke by church and secular authorities, intimidation, imprisonment, physical harm, torture, and even death. *The threat to voice was and is enormous.* Many important ideas and issues arise. The discussion is a study in the crosscurrents of church history. The use of voice by women saints placed their relationships and their lives at risk. Relationality and survival were jeopardized. The following comments heard in this group are representative:

"They [the women saints] seem brainy and witty. They are a lot more than docile, loving women. They were fulfilling many more roles than 'bearer of children.'"

"What struck me the most was survival. The church felt that to survive it needed to put women down. A lot of times I think women feel that if they're to survive, they have to play a role which is humble, quiet and not assertive. Somehow, we women feel that survival means we have to be quiet. Until we grab the power back and say, 'no,' survival means we all have to stand up and be assertive, nothing will change. A lot of us see our survival as through someone else, not as on our own.

As long as we continue to think that's how to survive, that's exactly how we survive. Instead, we have to keep our own power and empower ourselves. That's where survival is going to come from."

"There are many women today who have acquired a sense of independence through financial independence and are no longer silent, but I think it's only through their ability to take care of themselves independent of any man. That independence gives them the sense of power to speak out and not to remain silent."

"Economic independence seems to be a factor in women's ability to take stands."

The groups look also at the aspects of faith development in the women saints. What are the common themes of the religious history of women saints? Solitude, which seems to be a form of separation from society, emerges as crucial. Meditation and prayer are essential. Community is vital. Mission is central. These same themes of solitude, community, and mission are evident in the history of women's religious orders. The themes of women's spirituality revealed in the lives of women saints are as follows:

❖ Attendance to one's inner voice through *solitude* and *contemplation and prayer.*
❖ *Attendance* to the voice of God in Scripture, and in the teaching and history of the church.
❖ Attentive *listening* to the voices of others in community.
❖ *Engagement* with others and the world through mission with and advocacy for others.

The lives of these women saints reveal a constant effort to develop and use their voices despite threats to voice and life. These women saints sought relationship with God, reality, and others. They pursued relationality. They developed agency and used their power with and for the benefit of others. Their lives and teachings reveal the themes of the research on agency, power, and voice development: relationality, tension in voice use, and use of power in concert with and for others.

Women's Voices and the Church—Linking Past and Present

From our historical inquiry thus far, it is evident that forces have worked to suppress women's voices. When I look at the psychological and historical evidence, I see tragedy and I feel anger. I identify with the strength of the women who have been leaders in the church. I see clearly the forces that suppress women's voices. Yet how hard it is to recognize and fight these forces. We as women are culturally informed and shaped. That is why it is helpful to identify these forces in history and then look to our present reality.

In voice retrieval, certain questions must be asked

regarding the lives and voices of women saints and women today:

❖ What forces encouraged the saint's voice?
❖ What forces have, with or without intent, encouraged or suppressed your voice?
❖ What is characteristic of these faithful women's voices?
❖ Are there similarities to the previously listed characteristics of women's preaching?
❖ Does the church "hear" certain qualities in women's voices and screen out other qualities?
❖ Does the church affirm or sanctify certain characteristics in women's voices and condemn others?

These are vital questions if we are to hear the voices of women in history and in the present.

No, it does not surprise me when people cannot remember women's voices. The work of voice retrieval with women and congregations must begin with the history of women's voices, past and present. To bring the work into present reality, each participant is asked to recall a woman who influenced her spiritually. The group begins to remember—one memory triggers another. As we remember and talk together, the voices of women are heard. In time, it is evident that, indeed, many women conveyed important spiritual truths. The voices of those women, which had been lost, are retrieved and heard anew.

Women preachers and women in the church engaged in voice retrieval examine memories of how their voices were encouraged or discouraged by the church in childhood. Some of the questions discussed are:

❖ What did the church teach about being a good Christian girl?
❖ How was this message conveyed?
❖ Did good Christian girls ask questions?
❖ Did good Christian girls argue?

❖ Did good Christian girls talk much in church or school or home?

In our discussion, women realize the loss of voice in childhood. Girls who had voices as children lose them in their passage to adulthood, taught by others that to give voice is dangerous and will threaten relationship. Slowly, in the security of relationship to each other, women recall the voices that influenced them and begin to retrieve their own voices. The women ask each other, What were you taught about God? What did it mean to be a good girl? A faithful woman? We ponder these questions probing our memories.

Beginning with the discussion of women saints, the women become more aware of the loss of their own voices in adolescence and the risks to voice in adulthood. The discussion of the psychological research and the sharing of personal experience give insight into the complex issues of voice loss and voice retrieval. The historical material on women saints and the church's response to them validates the struggle of women to give voice in the church in the past and the present. The goal is to increase each woman's awareness of the importance of her voice. As one woman seminarian put it,

> I am now very conscious of my voice and where and how I choose to use it. In every class, I stop and think, "I'm not speaking. What is holding me back? Do I have something I want to say? What is the risk in speaking here? Do I want to take the risk of using my voice? What is really important for me to give voice to in this discussion in this class?" I go through this thought process regularly now in classes, in meetings, even in conversations with people. It's like I have this new consciousness of my voice and my personal knowledge. I make conscious decisions about what I think and to what I will give voice.
>
> I was with a group discussing a very controversial issue last night at dinner. In the past, I probably would have kept quiet even though I disagreed with the pre-

dominant view. But this time I thought, "It's important for me to state my view—to use my voice to register my view." So I waited and then at a certain point I said that I held a different view and I stated my own ideas. I was clear that I didn't want to argue but I did want to state my own convictions. I think the group was surprised. We talked a bit more but didn't argue much. I think they will give some thought to what I said. It felt so important to choose to use my voice and to be heard. That kind of consciousness and behavior are new for me.

Personal awareness of voice is essential to voice retrieval, but so is greater awareness of the intentional or unintentional efforts of persons and institutions to suppress women's voices.

Recently, a theology seminar met with several leaders of the Protestant church in Ghana, West Africa. A woman student noted the absence of any women pastors among the leaders, and she asked the male leaders why no women were holding leadership positions in the denomination. The leaders responded to her question, but the meeting became very tense and formal. No other inquiries were discussed even though other students raised some.

Later students met to analyze the meeting with the church leaders. A male student said, "I did not appreciate the reaction to your question about the absence of women leaders." The woman seminarian asked, "Are you saying I should not have asked the question?"

"No," he responded, "but your question ended all further discussion with the leaders. It stopped discussion."

"Was that my fault?" asked the woman.

"No," he responded, "but I wish the discussion hadn't ended."

She answered, "I feel like you are telling me if I had kept quiet, the discussion wouldn't have ended. You're saying if I hadn't voiced my concern, the meeting would have gone on and been a positive discussion."

The male seminarian said, "I guess it sounds like that. I just wanted the discussion to continue and to get a chance to ask more questions."

The woman seminarian said, "It seems as if you blame me for the discussion ending. So, I should not use my voice because it might upset the church leaders. I did not end the discussion. The church leaders ended the discussion, and you're telling me I should keep quiet so they will talk to you."

The group began to see how easy it would be to blame the tension on the woman's question. The group could see how easily they could move in to wanting to inhibit the women's voices. A woman's voice had caused disruption, tension. The woman was at fault. She should not have given voice to a controversial topic. She should have kept quiet so the discussion could continue. The discussion would continue, but the topic of great concern to women would never be voiced.

Such consciousness of voice and use of voice is at the heart of the process of voice retrieval. In classes and in various educational settings, the focus is on:

❖ Gaining awareness of one's voice through discussion of memories, psychological research, church history, and personal experience.

❖ Entering into a process of voice retrieval with a group of women—women seminarians or women preachers or laywomen in the church.

Following participation in a voice retrieval group, many women seek ongoing support and resources for the increased use of voice. Some of the available resources are journal writing, spiritual direction, consultation with peers, and psychotherapy.

A format incorporating these elements of voice retrieval is presented in chapter 5.

CHAPTER 5

Retrieving Women's Voices

"A woman's tongue is more powerful than a man's brawn."
That is an African saying, so we women talk and talk and
talk.

—Mercy Amba Oduyoye
Feminist Theologian
Princeton Seminary

Retrieving Women's Voices: Perspective and Process

THE CHURCH'S MINISTRY WITH WOMEN MUST CENTER ON
enabling women to give voice, and that entails encouraging women to see, to hear, and to speak their perceptions regarding self, others, reality, and God. It is essential that women be assured of the church's attentiveness
in order to risk speaking forth. In the narrative account
of voice used on page 40, a woman seminarian describes
ambivalence about her voice as a singer. This is a
poignant example of chosen voice suppression and her
decision to retrieve and use her voice. The voices of
women preachers, teachers, counselors, leaders, and
singers are waiting to be retrieved and heard.

Having examined the ambivalence and tension experienced in preaching and having inquired into the congregational response of "resistance to women's voices," and

"selective listening," we come to the crucial question: What is to be done then?

There are two elements in the work of voice retrieval: *the retrieval of a woman's voice* and *the church's welcome of her voice.* In the chapters ahead we examine each. The following are some questions to focus the work of each.

The work of voice retrieval for women preachers
❖ How can a woman preacher address her ambivalence regarding voice use and the risks of voice authenticity?

❖ How can a woman preacher retrieve her voice and use her voice to preach more effectively?

The work of the church in voice retrieval
❖ How can congregations and the church welcome women's voices, that is, how can congregations listen attentively and openly so as to "hear" and "engage" with women's voices as preachers and leaders of the church?

To address these issues I have developed a methodology for voice retrieval based upon a process for counseling women discussed in the book *A Feminist Position on Mental Health* by Mary Ballou and Nancy Gabalac. Ballou and Gabalac propose a counseling format to counter the effects of what they call "harmful adaptation" in women. I have modified the counseling format to work with women in voice retrieval.

Countering Harmful Adaptation: A Process for Corrective Action

Step 1—Separation
A movement toward separation of the woman from the pervasive negative messages encourages her to tell

her own story to the counselor and to other women. As she tells her own story and hears others' stories, a greater sense of the reality of the world around her grows, as does her confidence in her ability to know what is real.

Step 2—Validation

In the storytelling process, the counselor works for validation of the woman's experience and helps her affirm her strengths, which may have been defined as weakness all of her life.

Step 3—Association

Association with other women is a crucial part of counseling. Women's groups should be available for women's affiliation and empowerment.

Step 4—Authorization

Authorization is learning to be strong and accountable for oneself. It does not mean being falsely independent but knowing oneself well enough to have boundaries and still recognize interdependency.

Step 5—Negotiation

The negotiation phase is the testing out, with the ongoing support of counselor and group, of these new behaviors and thoughts in the woman's day-to-day environment.

STEP 1—SEPARATION PHASE

For the woman preacher this step involves separating herself from situations and persons who, either consciously or unconsciously, try to stifle, inhibit, or intimidate her voice. It is important for the woman preacher to do an honest appraisal of the situations and people with whom she functions in the ministry. Messages of resistance to her voice may be subtle. One woman seminarian described an interaction with her pastor whom she held in high esteem:

> I preached last Sunday and then discussed the sermon Tuesday with my pastor. He has known me for many years and has watched my preaching develop over my years in seminary. He said, "I liked the way you used to preach before you went to seminary. You were softer and more gentle in your approach."

The woman seminarian went on to say,

> I think he meant that he liked my preaching better when I wasn't using my voice. In those early sermons, before this class made me conscious of my voice, I was very tentative in what I preached and how I preached. Now, I'm trying to use my voice in preaching by asserting my own understanding of the world and of the gospel. He said I've developed a hard edge in my preaching and he finds it a problem. He noted that he used to feel warm and affirming after I preached and now he doesn't. He said, also, that he had noticed that people weren't as enthusiastic in their responses to my preaching. People used to say my sermons were wonderful and they loved my preaching. Now they don't seem to be as "blown away" by my preaching.

I asked the student, "What do you make of this?" She said,

> I think he has a problem with my voice. I'm not preaching as a tentative, hesitant woman who needs reassurance. I'm making clear, strong statements and he's got a problem with that. I think he's the one with the problem. I'm trying to process his comments and find any valuable, concrete feedback, but I am clear I don't want to

change my voice to obtain his approval. I would have been crushed by his comments before this class made me conscious of my voice and how people respond to it.

This woman's assessment of her pastor's reaction to her preaching indicates very well the subtleties and intricacies of assessing who welcomes and who negates a woman's voice. Often, the person who is in a supportive, caring relationship to a woman preacher or who is "mentoring" her can be giving negative messages regarding voice.

So, in the separation phase, a woman preacher assesses the situations and persons with whom she functions and analyzes how her voice is heard. Is there resistance to her voice in this place? Or with this person? Colleagues, teachers, members of the congregation, church leaders, family members—all need to be viewed honestly and evaluated in terms of receptivity or resistance to the woman's voice.

A group of women preachers is an essential resource in this process. Assessment of the response of others to one's voice can be attempted individually and can be fruitful. However, within a group, there is the opportunity to share anecdotes, questions, and ambiguities. Women assist one another in identifying resistance to voice. The woman seminarian quoted above participated in a preaching class that incorporated the voice retrieval process. The group helped each woman examine various responses to her preaching and her voice use. The women began to detach themselves from situations and persons who responded negatively to their voices. This separation from persistent negative response was a matter of mental attitude and physical proximity. The woman preachers invested less time, energy, and emotional exchange with persons and situations that would give negative messages regarding voice. Obviously, sometimes that was difficult if a supervisor or colleague were involved. However, awareness of the repeated negative reactions to voice use was a major step toward reducing the impact of negative response on the woman preacher. This awareness was exemplified in the woman seminarian's account of her pastor's evaluation of her preaching.

So, the first step for women preachers is the separation phase in which persistent negative responses to voice are identified and separation from them is undertaken.

STEP 2—VALIDATION PHASE

In this phase, the woman preacher is assisted in naming her experiences concerning voice use, voice reception, and reality. She gives voice to her perceptions of situations, relationships, spiritual understanding, interpretations of Scripture, church history, and church teaching. *Her* perceptions, insights, and voice are validated. *Her voice has integrity because it comes from within her no matter how anyone responds to it.*

The process of validation is crucial for women preachers to gain awareness of and use of voice. This phase goes hand in hand with the separation phase as women gain greater awareness of voice, its use and responses to it. Each woman's voice is validated again and again and again. Here, as in step 1, a group is vital. A woman preacher can seek validations of her voice with various chosen individuals she trusts. However, individual validation is not nearly the resource that a group engaged in validating each woman's voice can be.

In the validation phase, the perceptions, views, ideas, and so forth for which women have been criticized previously may be revealed as accurate and significant. The attitudes a woman may have seen as liabilities or weaknesses may in fact be signs of her wisdom and strength.

To return to the woman seminarian and her pastor, the group validated her insight regarding the pastor's response to her preaching. They asked her to talk more about her preaching and his responses in the past and in the present. Where another group might have assumed that if the pastor said she was less effective in her preaching now, then she was less effective and had better change her preaching, this group of women preachers validated and encouraged the woman in her goal of voice retrieval.

STEP 3—ASSOCIATION PHASE

The association phase generates confidence in the power of women to welcome and nurture insight, growth, and strength in one another. Many women preachers have relationships with persons whom they find affirm their individual growth. Women seek to associate themselves with individuals who affirm and nurture them, but they are often not discriminating enough in the relationships they seek or invest in. During this phase, each woman will test the reality of the group's welcome of her voice.

Experience with women preachers indicates that each group usually includes women at various stages of voice retrieval. In the association phase, women build trust that one woman will not criticize another woman for her timidity or her forcefulness. The women are allowed to inquire and encourage but not push one another. Each woman and each woman's voice is validated in whatever form it takes because it is *hers,* not because the group welcomes it. The women in the group build a history of experiencing association and voice welcome.

The association phase has to take time—at least six sessions. Time builds the corporate experience, the corporate history that leads a woman away from those who negate or inhibit her voice and toward the rewards of voice retrieval.

STEP 4—AUTHORIZATION PHASE

In this phase, the women preachers concentrate not just on retrieving voice but on being authorized to use it. Through the process of giving voice in the group, the woman literally gets to know herself and her voice better. She begins to acquire greater self-awareness and self-consciousness in voice use. Initially, many women experience increased inner tension and even anxiety during this phase. They need to be reassured that each woman's pace of voice retrieval and voice authorization is her own. No one knows the risks, both personal and professional, that each woman may encounter There is no right pace, only *her* process of voice retrieval.

In this phase, deliberation takes place as women recount increased voice consciousness and voice use with various individuals and groups. The group consistently responds with attention and respect for each woman's situation. Such response is invaluable in authorizing each woman's voice.

This phase seems to be characterized by humor and joy. The groups with which I have worked have taken on a very positive energy at this point. Trust has been building and the women look forward to the meetings. One hears comments like, "I couldn't wait to tell you all about what happened in this meeting this week," or "Wait till I tell you what Pastor Smith said and how I handled it," or "You won't believe what I did in this week's sermon." The women have seen one another changing and are delighted with the ever-strengthening voices they hear from one another. The voice retrieval process is understood, and they are well into the work. As one woman said:

It is as if I have this whole new understanding of the way I function and the way people respond to me. I used to come away from a meeting or conversation angry or depressed and not know why. Now I'll ask: "Was I heard? Was my voice received? Was there resistance to my voice and that's why I'm angry?" At other times, I realize I didn't use my voice even if I spoke words. Now, at the best of times, I can stop myself in a situation and think, "Do I want to use my voice here? To what would I give voice?"

Just as with the other phases, this phase continues throughout the life of the group. The process of authorizing one another goes on and on becoming more potent and more delightful for each member and the group.

STEP 5—NEGOTIATION PHASE

For women preachers, I believe this phase involves testing voice and consciously negotiating the costs and benefits of use of voice. In this phase, the women have gained familiarity with voice retrieval and are making more conscious decisions about voice use. They understand the dynamics of resistance to voice and readily identify them. In this phase, women preachers attempt to make conscious decisions about and take risks with voice in preaching. Women preachers discuss how to alter sermon preparation so as to nurture voice. In addition to their own ideas, members of the group discuss the recommendations to preachers, which are found in chapter 6.

Women preachers work very hard in this phase to negotiate voice use in sermon development and delivery. They recognize the risks entailed in the relationship to the congregation and the relationship to colleagues. What is said in the sermon and how it is said are discussed in detail. Sermons by women that are currently in progress or have been recently preached are discussed.

The group plays a vital role in reassuring the woman preacher as she articulates ideas that seem to her to be outrageous or nontraditional or overly personal. The authorization of the woman's voice in relationship to God, to Scripture, to church, and to reality is a constant effort. As they give voice to their deepest convictions of faith, most women in the groups experience new insight and new energy spiritually, which in turn infuse their preaching with new life. The hunger to speak of God and to hear of each other's ideas and experiences makes the groups fertile soil in which faith seems to grow deeper and fuller. This negotiation phase is a spiritually rich one. Many mentioned this spiritual growth and excitement in evaluations of the voice retrieval groups.

The women preachers came to see the significance of voice retrieval and its use in their spiritual lives. Many women spoke of prayerfully seeking God's guidance and strength in their voice use. Others mentioned the phrase, "To bear witness to what we have seen and heard," as the Gospel writers did.

In the negotiation phase, each woman identifies certain times in preaching and in her day-to-day life where she might choose to use or not use her voice. She contemplates what is at risk in choosing to use her voice. One woman decided to work on giving voice with a church executive for whom she worked. She assessed with the group various professional decisions that she and her boss would be discussing. She talked about her own views and how to articulate them (i.e., discerning her voice and then using her voice in the group). She noted what she would risk in using her voice with her supervisor:

❖ Being labeled pushy and insensitive
❖ Being seen as disagreeing with him
❖ Being seen as wrong

❖ Being seen as disloyal or unsupportive of the executive personally and/or organizationally
❖ Being evaluated negatively in her annual performance evaluation
❖ Being disliked or not appreciated or not respected
❖ Being bypassed for promotion
❖ Being left out of crucial meetings and discussions

The group listened to her, validated her perceptions, and encouraged her deliberations as a prelude to making a decision about voice use. She experienced the group authorizing her and proceeded to make conscious decisions about voice use. This is negotiation of voice use. She came back to the group to discuss the event afterward. It was a time to debrief, sometimes to celebrate and sometimes to commiserate. This woman had been helped in negotiating her voice use through the group's offer of support and suggestions of tactics.

It is particularly important in this phase for the group to remember that the woman is accountable to herself—not to the group. A woman may shift unconsciously toward courting the group's approval, which is just another form of losing her voice (i.e., altering her voice to please others).

The negotiation phase is the ongoing work of the group for women preachers and for laywomen who employ the voice retrieval method in the congregation. It can last as long as the group wants to continue meeting. I have worked with groups that met six times, groups that met daily for a week-long conference, and those that continue to meet monthly. Once a group understands and participates together in each phase, the work can continue in any time frame that benefits group members.

Once the foundational work is done, the ongoing work is fruitful as long as the tasks of separation, validation, association, authorization, and negotiation remain central to the group's process. This format for voice retrieval can be employed in many ways—groups or conferences for women preachers, a women's group within a congregation, a seminary class, an adult education class for men and women (see chapter 7 for an educational model for congregational use).

The voice retrieval concepts and format have been presented at a Feminist Theology Colloquium at Yale Divinity School. Faculty have found these concepts useful in encouraging the participation of women students in classes. Students report increased faculty sensitivity to voices of women past and present. Such responses have motivated the writing of this book so that voice retrieval might be a resource for women preachers, congregations, and educators. The implications for the field of pastoral studies are significant.

Finally, this voice retrieval method has been used in various settings—seminary, congregation, and conference—with very positive results. Women preachers, laywomen, and seminarians are enthusiastic about the process. They indicate it addresses the dynamics and tensions of preaching. Many preachers find they preach more creatively and effectively after participating in a voice retrieval effort as an individual and especially within a group.

Pastors and congregational groups participating in an educational program on voice retrieval have noted new receptivity and energy in the preaching ministry and women's participation in congregational life.

Perhaps more important than the process of voice retrieval itself is the intentionality it promotes in a woman. Self-awareness and voice awareness lead to a consciousness of power and resource in oneself. No matter what decisions are made regarding voice use, a woman experiences a new sense of power and control.

She becomes aware that it is her voice and her decision when and how to use it. This positive experience of power and autonomy replaces the feelings of anxiety and self-doubt. The woman's mental focus changes, and this change in itself has significant value. Self-confidence leads to more exciting and creative efforts in leadership and in preaching. Educators are very clear that a positive, confident mental attitude enhances intellectual endeavors. So, it is worth voice retrieval for women. The resurgence of women preachers engaged in voice retrieval corroborates this. Voice retrieval is a significant resource for women seeking to speak and preach more effectively.

CHAPTER 6

Voice Retrieval and Sermon Preparation

I began to see . . . a greater value lay in hearing and seeing from within that mysterious inner place, where the eyes and ears of the mind are insulated from the need to communicate to someone else what I experienced. The energy necessary to express myself to someone else seemed to have been conserved for the harder look, the keener hearing.

—From Fifty Days of Solitude *by Doris Grumbach*

IN HER 1994 BOOK, *FIFTY DAYS OF SOLITUDE*, DORIS GRUMbach writes of a self-imposed retreat from physical and verbal contact with a world she knows and loves in an effort to examine solitude. In exploring the nature and effects of solitude she asserts its positive impact on her ability to hear and speak with her own voice. Grumbach speaks of turning to solitude where she hopes to find the "voice, so often before styled or stilled entirely by what I thought others wanted to hear." Grumbach discusses what led her to this self-imposed fifty days of solitude. She refers to her rich, full life, the life of a gregarious woman, which was very pleasing. However, she became increasingly aware of the effect of a life of constant communication with others. Her journey into solitude demonstrated to her the effort necessary not only to maintain such communication but to stave off communication that was unwanted and perhaps detrimental. She seems to be saying that a life full of communication with others, appreciated or unappreciated others, requires energy of the individual. This expenditure of energy to maintain communication impairs the individual's ability to attend to an inner life and an inner knowledge and an inner voice. Her insights are relevant to the concepts of voice retrieval.

Up to this point, I have emphasized ways in which women can retrieve their voices through work with self and others to support voice. Grumbach's book illustrates another aspect of voice retrieval that is essential—the personal, internal work of voice retrieval. The internal work of voice retrieval necessitates personal commitment and regular periods of solitude to examine oneself, one's reality, and one's relationship to the world and to God.

This effort at personal attention to voice cannot be overemphasized. Without personal commitment to seek the solitude necessary in voice retrieval, no essential voice retrieval can take place in the individual. Self-consciousness, study, education, group work—all are resources, but they support the individual work. These resources alone cannot do the work of voice retrieval for the individual. The foundation of voice retrieval is personal, internal voice expression. Internal voice expression demands regular periods of solitude and attention. How does a preacher, who is consciously working to retrieve and encourage her voice, prepare for preaching?

Suggestions for Sermon Preparation

Some practical steps in sermon preparation will impact preaching effectiveness and authenticity. Voice retrieval is an interior, personal process best accomplished in dialogue with other women preachers as well as through the process that is described in this book. Experimenting with sermon preparation can enhance the work.

The crux of the preacher's task in sermon preparation is to *listen* to her own voice and to God's voice. Many women preachers in the groups and conferences described in this book find the idea of voice a new and exciting concept. These preachers not only have experienced the familial and cultural pressure to suppress their voices, but also have been cautioned in preaching classes about the dangers of personalizing preaching. As a result, many women speak of trying consciously to avoid any personal perspective in sermon preparation. Women preachers recount hours of research and exegesis in order to feel adequate in sermon writing. I believe this is symptomatic of the tension women feel about listening to and using their own voices. Listening to and using one's own voice differs from becoming personal in sermons. Listening to one's own voice involves affirming knowledge of God and the reality of our world. It is to seek to understand what God has revealed and continues to reveal. It is the fruit of a life of faith.

Resources for the Process of Hearing One's Own Voice

Solitude
Meditation
Journal writing
Spiritual direction
Engagement with the creative arts (e.g., music, drama, literature, etc.)
Dialogue with others
Intimate conversation
Psychotherapy
Dreaming
Experiencing other cultures

If a woman preacher is engaged in attentively hearing her own voice in her life of faith, she will find that she has a foundation for the task of negotiating use of her voice in her preaching.

So, the first step in hearing one's own voice is a regular commitment of time and energy toward speaking and hearing within oneself. Assuming this foundation, I will move on now to the process of attending to one's voice in sermon preparation.

In the context of solitude and conscious nurture and retrieval of one's voice, I have some recommendations for women preachers as they prepare to preach.

Recommendations for Sermon Preparation

The Listening

Try to come to this work with a calm, fresh mind.

❖ Once a text for preaching is assigned, read the scripture passages aloud several times, varying the voice in volume, pitch, and speed.

❖ Allow yourself to read in various ways in order to emphasize different aspects of the passage each time. Also, vary the emotional tone and emphasis of your reading.

❖ What have you noticed about the passage through reading it aloud? What strikes you intellectually, emotionally, spiritually? Jot down words and phrases that come to mind. Try to set your mind free.

❖ Close your eyes and ask yourself what images come to mind after hearing the passage. Let yourself envision in silence for a few minutes and then note any images or feelings that were stimulated.

The goal in this phase is to stimulate the mind, psyche, and spirit through listening and envisioning.

Allow your thoughts to roam as freely as possible. Do not try to think rationally or thematically or in an ordered way. This phase is like holding a handful of seeds and scattering them on fertile soil. Your psyche and spirit are doing unconscious work. Trust them. Your job is to provide the rich soil. Listen to yourself and to God. Take a break of two to twenty-four hours.

Reference

Come to this work with a fresh, calm mind and spirit. Do not misunderstand the title of this phase and assume you are to do academic research. Rather, it is a phase of research into your subconscious treasure trove to associate the scripture's message with your experience of God and reality. The goal is to bring the richness of your experience to consciousness and to voice it to yourself.

❖ Read the scripture aloud several times again. Make note of any words, images, or thoughts that occur to you. Do not stay with this task too long and do not begin writing the sermon. Allow yourself only ten minutes for this exercise.

❖ What fairy tales, children's stories, fables, or myths come to mind when you read and ponder these scripture texts? You may think this is a strange question, but children's literature often deals with powerful human themes. Myths and fables are the refined oral tradition of humanity and, similar to fairy tales, depict issues and forces central to a human reality. Recalling these tales will take you back to an earlier time in your life and significant human realities like abandonment, provision, guilt, and causality.

Pondering these issues can be informative for the preacher prior to writing the sermon. These themes

reconsidered from an adult's perspective seem to illuminate the Scriptures, reinforcing and intensifying the
power of the events, teachings, and promises of faith. The
task here is to let your mind go with memories and feelings. Give yourself time before you reach for paper to
record an idea. Your mind will be doing its work of sorting through your memory file, pulling out bits and pieces
of what it remembers and knows. It will do the retrieving
and integrating. Your job is to listen to yourself. Trust
your mental capacity. It is a tremendous resource, and
you probably do not provide enough silence or attention
to benefit from it. When you feel ready, make notes.

❖ Does the scripture remind you of any play, poetry,
   musical composition, painting, or similar work? This
   is an attempt to relate the scripture to any artistic
   encounters. When I teach, I refer to artists as speaking
   the language of the soul. Artists are seeking to communicate their knowledge of reality and humanity
   with us. Their perspective—their truth—can be a
   powerful stimulus to our own creative efforts in sermon writing.

❖ Think about the historical and cultural settings of the
   scripture. How do they relate to the passage? Does the
   scripture remind you of any other time or event in
   history? What about the world scene today? Do you
   see any similarities?

❖ Meditate on your own human relationships past and
   present. Are there any similarities to or differences
   from the issues presented in the scripture you are
   using (e.g., Jesus speaks of forgiving a brother seventy
   times seven times; for what do I need to be forgiven in
   terms of my relationship to my boss or my children?)?

❖ Take a blank sheet of paper and start writing words
   that come to mind. Put the words all over the page.
   See what emerges.

All of this work is meant to be done in a leisurely, relaxed mode. Think of your mind working at the pace of a gently flowing stream. Do not stop. Keep moving, but move slowly the way a stream caresses and moves over each rock. Over time, you will come to trust that this process will stimulate thought and voice. The mental journey takes from one to two hours, and it is a rich resource for sermon content.

Research

This is the time for the exegetical work. In this phase, you consult the standard references of sermon preparation (i.e., commentaries, texts, concordances, lexicons, etc.). Do not forget to inquire into the historical and cultural realities surrounding the scriptures. Read, study, and think. Do not start writing the sermon either in your head or on paper. Write notes, but do not decide on themes. Your mind is still surveying the landscape. Do not focus on one part of the scene.

This is a time for mental expansiveness. The memories, the inner voice, the imagination, the Holy Spirit, and the mind are all in conversation. Push yourself to keep hearing, seeing, learning, pondering. Some preachers are so anxious that they stop after one or two ideas present themselves, relieved to think they have something of value to say in the sermon. Do not stop your exploration phase too early. Your mind is sifting and winnowing for you. Think of it as you would contemplate a meal in a cafeteria. Do not settle for the first thing you encounter. Scan all of the possible choices and see what you feel like putting on your plate.

You may think that these recommendations are too simple to be of any real value in producing sermons of intellectual depth. In fact, this whole process is meant to take you into the richer territory of your memory and mind. Using random thought rather than deductive thinking will promote creativity and stimulate your internal voice. God has been teaching and informing you spiritually throughout your life, not just through school and church. God has been present through every encounter with reality, speaking to you in each moment. You need to open your ears to hear God's voice past and present. You also need to loosen your tongue to give voice to your knowledge of God.

It may seem that the sermon preparation has taken a lot of time so far. In fact, phases one to three will probably take two to three hours in all. However, it is helpful to do the work over two to three days so that there can be space between phases for your mind to work unconsciously while you are doing other things. I recommend doing phases one to three early in the morning or before bedtime each day. Set aside thirty to forty minutes each day to do the mental work. The research phase is the exception. It may take several hours, depending on your level of effort. Most of us feel we never do enough research before writing the sermon.

Percolating

You may have guessed the origin of this phase's name. Before the era of drip coffeemakers, the primary method for making coffee was in a percolator in which boiling water bubbled up and over coffee grounds again and again and again until a dark, rich coffee was brewed. This phase of sermon preparation is quite similar. The psyche and spirit go through a process of bubbling up and over the mental data, which have been implanted or retrieved in the previous three phases. This is a largely unconscious process, and you must learn to trust that it is going on constantly while you are doing other things such as driving, walking, eating, conversing, sleeping, and so on. You can encourage the process through prayer. Here is one preacher's prayer:

> There is important work being done at all times by my psyche and my mind. That work of noticing, of taking in, of analyzing, of integrating is a rich resource in my life. That work helps me "know" my reality, myself, and God. I want to pay special attention to my mind and psyche in these next few days. I want my mind and psyche to speak to me regarding these scriptures. Do the work of integrating all of the threads that have emerged in the meditating, researching, and free-associating that have been done. Mind, heart, soul, and psyche, speak to me. Holy Spirit, speak to me through them.

The preacher's job, then, is to be prepared to listen to the product of the percolating. Be prepared to have thoughts come into your consciousness at odd times. Let your mind welcome whatever images, thoughts, words, or phrases occur. I have found that carrying several three-by-five-inch cards in my datebook is a good way to be prepared to jot a quick note to myself in the middle of a meeting or cooking or some other activity. Or you may prefer to use a little tape recorder because revelation may strike in the car. For many people, this process of attending to the internal voice is unfamiliar, so don't be discouraged if it seems awkward or unproductive at first. Every person has an internal voice. You are welcoming a new you into your consciousness, your conscious life, and your work.

In fact, once attendance to your mind's percolating has become a regular part of your life, you can employ it as a great creative resource in other areas such as designing an educational event, figuring out a relationship, or making a decision. Within the field of psychology, this mental integrating process is often referred to as ego functioning, based on Sigmund Freud's theories that asserted that the mental functions of gathering data, sorting data, conceptualizing, analyzing, and integrating were done by the ego. Percolating goes on all the time. The challenge is to become more conscious of its messages and attend to them in sermon preparation and in life.

Pray that you might be more attentive in listening to your inner voice. Pray that the Holy Spirit will inspire, enlighten, and inform you through your internal voice and in every other possible way. Then, trust God to do it.

This approach is *not* intended to reinforce undisciplined or uninformed sermon preparation. Often, preachers find it difficult to take the time and energy necessary for sermon preparation. Given the demands of the ministry, it is easy to fall into poor habits of sermon preparation. The emphasis on the percolating phase should not be interpreted as indicating that percolating is more important than the research or free-associative phase. I am putting extra emphasis on the percolating phase because it is an often overlooked resource.

So—pay attention to the percolation phase. Make time for it.

Writing the Sermon

Now, you are ready to proceed to writing the sermon manuscript. I believe a full manuscript of a sermon is necessary even if you preach from notes alone. The manuscript preparation disciplines your thoughts and words. As you rework a manuscript, keep giving voice to the sermon through speaking it aloud either alone or with another.

Sermon Delivery

Here the big word is PRACTICE. So many good sermons are less effective because too little emphasis has been given to delivery. Read it, talk it, and speak it until the sermon is within you. Then trust God to use your voice and person in the preaching event.

In addition to the voice retrieval process and practice, I urge preachers to contract for several sessions with a voice coach, someone in drama and/or music. Sermon delivery can be significantly improved through expanding vocal range. Consciousness of voice pitch, timbre, inflection, and audibility will benefit any preacher. Vocal exercises are a great resource to incorporate in your preaching regimen and preparation.

Exploring different ways to use your voice in the sanctuary where you will be preaching is beneficial to sermon delivery. I spoke earlier of preaching being analogous to swimming in that one learns to use one's body in a new medium—for the swimmer the medium is water; for the preacher the medium is the space of the sanctuary. So take the time to become familiar with that medium.

Move and speak in that pulpit, in that sanctuary. Speak loudly. Speak softly. Speak slowly. Speak quickly. Reading psalms aloud is a great exercise, for the psalms cover the range of human feeling and experiences. Become familiar with the sanctuary and the sound and range of your voice in it. Exercise your voice regularly in this space. Such familiarity has positive associations for you and will enhance your preaching.

Whatever you choose to do, do not neglect the area of sermon delivery. Communication is not a cerebral or solo event. It involves the speaker, the hearer, and the environment. Attend to all of them.

Having preserved the practices of voice retrieval and sermon preparation, we come to the role of hearer and collective hearers, the church welcoming women's voices. What is entailed in the hearer and the church addressing the resistance to women's voices so as to actively attend to women's voices? For that is the vision—a church no longer resisting women's voices, but welcoming women's voices.

But for a vision to take shape there needs to be a process to implement it. And so, in the next chapter I turn to an educational program to help congregations join in the process of retrieving and welcoming women's voices.

CHAPTER 7

Welcoming Women's Voices

A holy people and blameless race
wisdom delivered from a nation of oppressors.
She entered the soul of a servant of the Lord,
and withstood dread kings with wonders and signs.
She gave to holy people the reward of their labors;
she guided them along a marvelous way,
and became a shelter to them by day,
and a starry flame through the night.
She brought them over the Red Sea,
and led them through deep waters;
but she drowned their enemies,
and cast them up from the depth of the sea. . . .
they sang hymns, O Lord, to your holy name,
and praised with one accord your defending hand;
for wisdom opened the mouths of those who were mute,
and made the tongues of infants speak clearly.

—Wisdom of Solomon 10:15-19, 20b-21

An Educational Program for Faithful People

THIS PROGRAM IS DESIGNED FOR USE WITH WOMEN AND MEN
in churches and seminaries. It has been used in various
settings with groups interested in encouraging and

welcoming women's voices. I am grateful to St. John's Episcopal Church in North Guilford, Connecticut, the College of Preachers in Washington, D.C., and Carolyn Hardin Engelhardt of the Vieth Resource Center at Yale Divinity School for their assistance in formulating the program.

A Word to the Program Leader

To lead this program, you will need:

❖ To be a good colearner with your participants.
❖ To bring a listening and inquiring heart to this educational work.
❖ To read *Wrestling with the Patriarchs: Retrieving Women's Voices in Preaching,* chapters 1–6, on which this educational program is based.
❖ To use this leader's guide, making adjustments so it fits your group's particular goals and resources.

Program Setting

Try to establish a relaxed atmosphere through the room arrangement, refreshments, name tags if needed, and so forth. Here are some possible settings:

❖ A room similar to a family recreational room or living room where people can sit comfortably and talk together easily is preferable.
❖ No tables or desks are needed; try to avoid a classroom type of setting.
❖ The group will need to break into pairs or smaller groups at times for discussion so the setting should include access to other space where small groups can talk together.

❖ The meeting room for the program should have either a chalkboard or a large paper tablet where the leader can write down group comments noted as part of the program.

Group Guidelines

The leader should discuss with the group any guidelines they wish to set for their work together. The following are some suggestions:

1. Because the focus of the program is on retrieving and welcoming women's voices, it is important that participants listen very carefully to one another.
2. Each participant should make a deliberate effort to formulate individual ideas and voice them in the group. Participants should encourage one another to speak, thus creating a positive climate for women's voices.
3. Because each session is based on the preceding sessions, the participants are strongly urged to plan to attend *all* sessions. A participant who misses more than one session may choose to drop out of the program rather than try to catch up and perhaps distract the group.
4. A firm starting and ending time should be established although participants may come early and stay late for discussion or socializing.
5. It is important that all group participants agree that this group is not a place to debate the issues of resistance to voice or voice retrieval. Such discussion is valid, but that is not the intent of the program and will reduce the program's effectiveness in welcoming women's voices. Rather, the program is geared to persons committed to retrieving and welcoming women's voices.

Program Objectives

The leader should talk with the group about their expectations. The leader can share the following objectives with the group and add any additional objectives they suggest:

1. To experience a faith community that respects and welcomes the voices of all persons especially, at this time, the voices of women.
2. To examine the concept of one's voice as a gift from God to praise God, to share one's knowledge of God, and to further God's work in the world.
3. To come to understand the conscious and unconscious processes that affect one when one uses one's voice.
4. To seek to learn about women's voices through examining concepts of voice formation in women and through studying the lives of women saints and leaders in the church.
5. To contemplate how the church might address resistance to women's voices.
6. To work together in encouraging women to use their voices and to examine how women's voices are received in this church.
7. To share hopes and plans for the church to be more welcoming of women's voices, locally and nationally.

SESSION 1

Objectives

❖ To identify our own experience with women's voices/leadership and to recognize what we learned from them.

❖ To review some information that describes the preaching of women and men, noticing similarities and differences and discussing our own experience of the way we listen to women in our lives.

❖ To become familiar with the expectations and form of this educational program.

Gathering Time

The group may wish to gather for refreshments or a meal together with the understanding that the program will begin promptly at a set time.

Orientation

Welcome by the leader or leaders. The leader hands out a summary sheet and shares potential goals of the series, guidelines for group time together, and expectations regarding assignments and attendance.

Opening Meditation 5 MINUTES

The group gathers and sits in a circle if possible. The leader asks for several minutes of silent prayer, closing with the following prayer, which she says aloud:

> Open our ears that we might hear,
> Open our eyes that we might see,
> Open our lips that we might speak,
> O God. Amen.

Introductions 15 MINUTES (TOTAL GROUP)

Starting with the leaders, go around the group introducing yourselves, perhaps saying also what it took for you to get here (What I left at home?) and what you hope to gain from attending these sessions.

Part One 10 MINUTES (PAIRS)

Ask persons to move into pairs.

After moving into pairs, ask persons to remember in silence women who spoke to them of God when they were children. What messages were they given? Think of how these women taught about God or spiritual convictions.

Now tell partners about these memories.

Part Two 20 MINUTES (TOTAL GROUP)

In total group, make four charts:

1. Characteristics of women you recalled;
2. Ways each woman shared her knowledge of God and her spiritual teaching;
3. Ways people responded to the women;
4. Ways the women received support for sharing their knowledge of God and spiritual teaching.

Part Three 20 MINUTES (TOTAL GROUP)

The leader shares data on preaching of men and women and the evidence of cultural resistance to women's voices as presented in chapter 2 of *Wrestling with the Patriarchs*. Group discusses the material.

Assignment 10 MINUTES

The leader asks the group what they want to keep thinking about in light of tonight's session. The leader distributes the assignment sheet (see Assignment #1 in Appendix) and discusses any questions about the assignment.

Closing Meditation 10 MINUTES

The leader asks the group to stand in a circle and join hands. Each person is asked to say one word that she or he voices from this session's experiences. The leader or leaders speak first. After all have spoken a word the leader prays in a clear, bold voice, inviting the group to repeat the prayer after her in clear, bold voices (the leader prays the following prayer, then the group repeats it):

> Open our lips that
> We might praise
> You, O God. Amen.

SESSION 2

Objectives

❖ To examine the experiences of some women in voice/leadership in history to explore what we might learn from them.

❖ To become familiar with some information about men and women preaching.

Opening Meditation 5 MINUTES

The group gathers and sits in a circle if possible. The leader asks for several minutes of silent prayer, closing with the following prayer that she says aloud:

> Open our ears that we might hear,
> Open our eyes that we might see,
> Open our lips that we might speak,
> O God. Amen.

Orientation 5 MINUTES

The leader invites the participants to share any insights and observations since last week, what it took for them to get to this session.

Part One 15 MINUTES (TOTAL GROUP)

Three participants share their reports about women saints or leaders.

Part Two 15 MINUTES (TOTAL GROUP)

Make four charts with the same titles as last week. Add to the charts based on what was heard about the women in the reports.

Part Three 10 MINUTES (TOTAL GROUP)

Ask group members to make observations about what they do or do not see of compliance, assertiveness, power, authenticity, determination, outspokenness, reforming and political activity in the lives of the women in the reports. List these words and phrases on a board for all to see.

Part Four 20 MINUTES (TOTAL GROUP)

The leader presents information about women saints or leaders suffering rejection, rebuke, intimidation regarding their writings, teachings and actions. As discussed in chapter 4, rarely was the response of church authorities consistently positive.

Part Five 15 MINUTES (TOTAL GROUP)

Post charts from last week beside the charts just made. Ask the group to make any observations or share any insights they may have.

Part Six 10 MINUTES (TOTAL GROUP)

Ask the group to think about the implications of these ideas for our experience in the church and for how we hear women's voices.

Assignment 5 MINUTES

Give assignment handout (see Assignment #2 in Appendix).

Closing Meditation

The leader asks the group to stand in a circle and join hands. Each person is asked to say one word that she or he voices from this session's experiences. The leader or leaders speak first. After all have spoken a word the leader prays:

> Open our lips that
> We might praise you,
> O God. Amen.

SESSION 3

Objectives

❖ To hear and discuss reports on the lives of various women saints
❖ To examine how each woman's voice developed
❖ To see what encouraged each woman saint's voice and what discouraged that voice
❖ To discuss how each woman saint used her voice
❖ To discover the threats women saints encountered in using their voices
❖ To look for common characteristics and themes in the lives and voices of women saints.

Opening Meditation 5 MINUTES

The group gathers and sits in a circle if possible. The leader asks for several minutes of silent prayer, closing with the following prayer, which she says aloud:

> Open our ears that we might hear,
> Open our eyes that we might see,
> Open our lips that we might speak,
> O God. Amen.

Orientation 10 MINUTES

Hear any insights and observations from the group about the topic of the series. Ask whether people have any observations from the workplace, meetings, or family members.

Part One 30 MINUTES (TOTAL GROUP)

Hear reports on women saints or leaders.

Part Two 30 MINUTES (TOTAL GROUP)

Complete charts as in session 2.

Part Three 30 MINUTES (TOTAL GROUP)

Hand out this list of questions for group reflections and sharing:

1. Have we seen compliance, obedience, humility, self-sacrifice, or other dominant themes in research on women saints? What data do we have to support these depictions of women?
2. Why might church historians have emphasized these qualities?
3. Did any of the women saints exhibit the quality of assertiveness? Were any considered powerful or influential women? By whom?
4. What was the relationship of each woman saint to her world (i.e., her town, her nation, etc.)?
5. Did any of the women saints suffer threats, intimidation, or rejection due to her teaching?

(*Note to leader:* Teresa of Avila, Catherine of Siena, and Hildegard of Bingen—all saints—suffered the threat of the label heretic. All were criticized by the church authorities for their teaching and work.)

Closing Meditation

The leader asks the group to stand in a circle and join hands. Each person is asked to say one word that she or he voices from this session's experiences. The leader or leaders speak first. After all have spoken a word the leader prays:

> Open our lips that
> We might praise you,
> O God. Amen.

SESSION 4

Objectives

❖ To hear about research on psychological development of girls and women, which indicates the vulnerability of voice and the focus on relationships.
❖ To explore the implications of this research for the church.
❖ To explore what attitudes exist within the congregation and what, if any, changes should be considered.

Opening Meditation 5 MINUTES

Repeat from previous sessions, or use a song, litany, or reading by a woman from history.

Orientation 15 MINUTES

Share insights, questions, what was left at home from the last week.

Part One 20 MINUTES (PAIRS)

Ask the group to divide and sit in pairs.
Ask the group to recall in silence a situation in which they chose to speak out or to use their voices and a situation in which they chose not to speak or give voice.
Ask the pairs to share their memories.
Ask participants to join in a circle, and if anyone wishes to share from reflections, do so.

Part Two 30 MINUTES (TOTAL GROUP)

The leader presents research on the psychological development of girls and women from chapter 3, emphasizing the vulnerability of voice in girls and their focus on relationship. The leader may note that there is probably a relationship between memories and history we have explored and these research findings.

Ask the group to mention any observations, insights, or questions about this research that they might like to consider further.

Part Three 30 MINUTES (TOTAL GROUP)

Provide the following questions on a board, and ask participants to choose those they would like to discuss:

❖ How do you listen to women's voices in the church?
❖ As an adolescent, how was your voice received or not received in your family?
❖ Where do you currently feel your voice is received or not received, heard or not heard?
❖ What might be the differences in men's and women's experiences on these matters?
❖ How can you work to welcome women's voices in your family? In your church?
❖ How can you learn to listen more attentively to women's voices?

Closing Meditation 10 MINUTES

The leader asks the group to stand in a circle and join hands. Each person is asked to say one word that he or she voices from this session's experiences. The leader or leaders speak first. After all have spoken a word the leader prays:

> Open our lips that
> We might praise you,
> O God. Amen.

SESSION 5

Objectives

❖ To identify ways in which both men and women are affected by the cultural resistance to women's voices.
❖ To practice using voice and identifying personal resistance to women's voices.
❖ To identify what participants would hope for in relation to this topic—in society, congregation, family, and so on.

Opening Meditation 5 MINUTES

Open the same way as sessions 1 through 3, or use a litany, prayer, song, or reading from a woman in history.

Orientation 10 MINUTES

Invite group members to share what they have thought about on this topic since the last session.

Ask group members to tell about their increasing consciousness of voice and resistance to women's voices.

Ask group members to share how they may have seen this concern affecting men as well as women.

Part One 30 MINUTES (SMALL GROUPS)

Divide the group into smaller groups of five or six people with men and women in each, if possible.

Provide a copy of material on the steps in the retrieval process: separation, validation, association, authorization, and negotiation.

Ask one woman in each group to give her thoughts on an issue of concern to the church at the local or national level according to the following process:

❖ In each group ask two women to do the retrieval steps together in preparation for one of the women sharing a concern about church life with the group.

❖ While they prepare, the rest of the group may wish to do the retrieval steps or discuss them.

❖ When the woman is ready to share her concern, she introduces her issue and invites group discussion. She participates as she wishes, giving voice as she decides. The woman partner who talked with her becomes a participant-observer in the group, listening and watching group members' reactions and the woman's behavior. The other three or four group members are asked to be aware of their own responses in the discussion, attempting to be more attentive to and encouraging of women's voices.

Part Two 15 MINUTES (TOTAL GROUP)

Stop the discussion in small groups to ask them to reflect together on their reactions and behavior. Ask the participant-observer to comment on her observations. Ask the woman practicing voice to comment on how she felt. Ask group members how they felt. Ask all persons to say what they learned and what they might do differently next time.

Part Three 15 MINUTES (SMALL GROUPS)

Divide into a men's group and a women's group. Ask each group to share their reactions to the small groups' experiences.

Part Four 5 MINUTES (TOTAL GROUP)

Ask the whole group to return to a circle. Ask if there are observations that people wish to share.

Assignment 5 MINUTES

Participants are to note in the time between sessions how they use their own voices and respond to women's voices at home, at work, and at church. They are to bring an observation to share at the next session.

Closing Meditation 10 MINUTES

The leader asks the group to stand in a circle and join hands. Each person is asked to say one word that she or he voices from this session's experiences. The leader or leaders speak first. After all have spoken a word the leader prays:

> Open our lips that
> We might praise you,
> O God. Amen.

SESSION 6

Objectives

❖ To identify ways in which both men and women are affected by the cultural resistance to women's voices.
❖ To practice using voice and identifying personal resistance to women's voices.
❖ To identify what participants would hope for in relation to this topic—in society, congregation, family, and so on.
❖ To review the work of the group, recognizing that this is the last session together.
❖ To list insights from the program and discuss hopes for change in the church.

Opening Meditation 5 MINUTES (TOTAL GROUP)

Open the same way as session 5.

Orientation 15 MINUTES (TOTAL GROUP)

Share insights, issues, and questions that arose in participants' reflections since last week.

Part One 30 MINUTES (INDIVIDUAL)

Provide a sheet of paper with the following questions on it with space for answers. Ask each person to respond privately.

1. What changes do I want to make in my own use of voice and in my response to women's voices?
2. What changes do I want to happen in this church to encourage women's voices and to make it less resistant to women's voices?

(*Note to leader:* See sample in the Appendix.)

Part Two 60 MINUTES (TOTAL GROUP)

Ask the group to share responses to the second question.

List as a group the next steps that might be appropriate, such as telling or writing about this group's explorations in a newsletter or through announcements during worship.

Save all the charts and items people have written about the changes they would like to see, and plan to put them in the offering plate at the next Sunday worship service as an offering to God of their hopes, goals, and comments. These can also be typed up and posted or published in the church newsletter.

Closing Meditation 10 MINUTES

The leader asks the group to stand in a circle and join hands. Each person is asked to say one word that she or he voices from this session's experiences. The leader or leaders speak first. After all have spoken a word the leader prays:

> Open our lips that
> We might praise you,
> O God. Amen.

EPILOGUE

It was a conscious choice to end this book by challenging the Christian community to commit itself to retrieving and welcoming women's voices. For too long, teachers and hearers of women's voices have convinced women that voice retrieval is the speaker's problem. No, voice loss and retrieval is a costly problem for the church. Resistance to women's voices keeps the church from living as the full, rich, dynamic creation the church is intended to be. The church must address the retrieval and welcoming of women's voices even as women must address it.

Do we as the church dare to envision a Christian community alive with the wisdom and creativity of women's voices? Do we as the church dare to embody the new household of faith in which women and men challenge and complement one another, each perspective enriching our faith? That is the vision and that is God's promise. We are to be the church in the new order of salvation. May we indeed dare to envision and embody it.

To that end, this book has introduced the issues and the process that can bring voice retrieval to the fore for women and for the church. We have examined the issues and dynamics that women experience in preaching. Drawing on congregational research, we have looked at perceived gender differences in preaching. Drawing on current psychological studies, we have sought to understand voice formation and voice loss. Utilizing the lives and voices of women saints and faithful women today, we have examined resistance to women's voices in the church in the past and present. We have considered a voice retrieval process for women preachers and for congregations.

Some readers will be enthusiastic in response to these ideas, and some will be critical. It is my hope that no matter what your reaction, you will let this book lead you to examine your receptivity to women's voices. If the concepts and issues I have presented provoke thought in you, I have succeeded in my primary intent— to foster inquiry. If inquiry leads to dialogue with others, I will be very pleased, for another voice is speaking and other voices are being heard. If inquiry and dialogue lead to greater openness, as they inevitably do, who knows what that could mean for the church.

APPENDIX

ASSIGNMENT #1

Reflect on the following issues, making notes about them:

1. List situations in which you use or do not use your voice.

2. What encourages you to speak or inhibits you from speaking?

3. How can you listen more attentively to women's voices?

4. What in our culture influences us not to listen to women's voices and spiritual knowledge?

5. On what subjects do we really pay attention to what women have to say?

6. What are the "cultural resistances" to "hearing" women's voices in the church? In the congregation? In the seminary? In church members?

7. In what way might you be resistant to hearing women's voices? When and where are you resistant to hearing women's voices? In what groups or communities are you resistant to hearing women's voices?

8. Please choose a woman saint or leader from church history and find out what you can about her in an encyclopedia of religion, a dictionary of church history, or other books at the local library. You may be able to find writings by these women. You may tell your group what you found in the life, teachings, and writings of this woman. Please be prepared to present an informal report of no more than five minutes in one of the upcoming sessions. Some persons will share each week.

ASSIGNMENT #2

1. Be prepared to share your report on a woman saint or leader if you have not already.

2. Reflect on these questions:

A) In your history with the church, how has your voice been expressed? Do you feel free to use your voice and to be verbally active in church committees and activities?

B) Has your voice been encouraged within the church in the past? In the present? How so?

C) Has your voice been inhibited or rejected in the church in the past? In the present? How so?

D) How do you see resistance to women's voices?

E) How do you perceive "selective" hearing to be occurring?

F) Do you believe "selective" hearing occurred in your experience in the past or in the present?

G) In what ways may you resist women's voices?

Worksheet for Session 6

1. What changes do I want to make in my own use of voice and in my response to women's voices?

2. What changes do I want to happen in this church to encourage women's voices and to make it less resistant to women's voices?

NOTES

Chapter 2: Gender and Preaching

1. This theological discussion draws on consultations with Byron Stuhlman, a scholar who has written extensively in the area of liturgics and pastoral theology.

2. From correspondence received from Byron Stuhlman.

Chapter 3: Voice Formation in Women Preachers

1. "Joining the Resistance," an address delivered to the Association of Women in Psychology, a subdivision of the American Psychological Association, Hartford, Conn., 1991.

2. Ibid.

3. Harvard Medical School Conference on the Psychological Development of Women and Girls (Boston, Mass., April 1993).

4. Ibid.

5. Ibid.

6. "Joining the Resistance."

7. Ibid.

8. Ibid.

9. Discussion of the Harvard/Stone Center research on the Psychological Development of Women and Girls, Harvard Medical School Conference.

10. "Joining the Resistance."

11. Jean Baker Miller, "The Development of Women's Sense of Self" in *Women's Growth in Connection* (New York: Guilford Press, 1991), pp. 11-27.

12. Janet L. Surrey, "The Self-in-Relation: A Theory of Women's Development," in *Women's Growth in Connection*, pp. 51-67.

Chapter 4: Faithfulness, Agency, and Voice Retrieval

1. Jean Baker Miller, "Women and Power," *Women's Growth in Connection* (New York: Guilford Press, 1991), p. 163.

2. Father John Julian, *A Lesson of Love* (New York: Walker and Co., 1988).

3. Katherine Moore, *She for God: Aspects of Women and Christianity* (London: Allison and Beasley Ltd., 1978), p. 50.

4. Julian, *A Lesson of Love,* author's preface.

5. Ibid., pp. 11-12.

6. Jesus Castellano, "Christian, Human, and Cultural Values in St. Teresa of Jesus," delivered at the *Edith Stein Symposium,* published in *Carmelite Studies* Series 4 (Washington: International Carmelite Studies Publications, 1987), p. 110.

7. Kieran Kavanaugh and Otilio Rodriguez, trans., *The Collected Works of St. Teresa of Avila* (Washington: ICS Publications, 1980), pp. 4-5.

8. Bonaventure Lussier, "Jungian Individuation and Contemplation in Teresa of Jesus," *Carmelite Studies,* Series 4 (Washington, D.C.: International Carmelite Studies Publications, 1987), pp. 272-73.

9. Ibid., pp. 269-70.

10. Ibid., p. 273.

11. Castellano, "Christian, Human, and Cultural Values," p. 8.

12. Joseph S. Chorpenning, *The Divine Romance: Teresa of Avila's Narrative Theology* (Chicago: Loyola University Press, 1992), p. 20.

13. *Vision, The Music of Hildegard of Bingen* (New York: Angel Records, 1995).

14. Columba Hart and Jane Bishop, eds., *Hildegard of Bingen, SCIVAS* (New York: Paulist Press, 1990), foreword.

15. *The New Catholic Encyclopedia,* vol. 3 (Washington, D.C.: Catholic University of America), p. 259.

16. Quotation from *The Dialogue* by Catherine of Siena, cited in notes prepared by participants in the series *Retrieving Women's Voices* (St. John's Episcopal Church: North Guilford, Conn., 1993).

17. *New Catholic Encyclopedia,* p. 259.

BIBLIOGRAPHY

Brown, Lyn Mikel, and Carol Gilligan. *Meeting at the Crossroads.* New York: Ballantine, 1992.

Brunn, Emilie Zum, and Georgette Epiney-Burgard. *Women Mystics in Medieval Europe.* New York: Paragon House, 1989.

Campbell, Camille. *Meditations with Teresa of Avila.* Santa Fe: Bear and Co., 1985.

Chorpenning, Joseph S. *The Divine Romance: Teresa of Avila's Narrative Theology.* Chicago: Loyola University Press, 1992.

Claremont de Castillejo, Irene. *Knowing Woman: A Feminine Psychology.* New York: Harper and Row, 1973.

Cross, F. L., ed. *The Oxford Dictionary of the Christian Church.* Oxford, England: Oxford University Press, 1977.

Debold, Elizabeth, Marie Wilson, and Idelisse Malavae. *Mother Daughter Revolution: From Betrayal to Power.* New York: Addison-Wesley Publishing Co., 1993.

Durka, Gloria. *Praying with Hildegard of Bingen.* Winona, Minn.: St. Mary's Press, 1991.

Flanagan, Sabina. *Hildegard of Bingen.* London and New York: Routledge, 1989.

Fox, Matthew. *Illuminations of Hildegard of Bingen.* Santa Fe: Bear and Co., 1985.

Gilligan, Carol, Nona P. Lyons, and Trudy J. Hanmer, eds. *Making Connections: The Relational World of Adolescent Girls at Emma Willard School.* Cambridge: Harvard University Press, 1989.

Gilligan, Carol, et al. *Mapping the Moral Domain.* Cambridge: Harvard University Press, 1988.

———. *Women, Girls, and Psychotherapy: Reframing Resistance.* New York: Harrington Park Press, 1991.

Glaz, Maxine, and Jeannes Stevenson Moessner, eds. *Women in Travail and Transition: A New Pastoral Care.* Minneapolis: Fortress Press, 1991.

Hildegard of Bingen. *Hildegard of Bingen's Book of Divine Work with Letters and Songs.* Matthew Fox, ed. Santa Fe: Bear and Co., 1987.
———. *Scivias.* Trans. Mother Columba Hart and Jane Bishop. New York: Paulist Press, 1990.

Jordan, Judith V., et al. *Women's Growth in Connection.* New York: Guilford Press, 1991.
Julian, Father John. *A Lesson of Love.* New York: Walker and Co., 1988.
Julian of Norwich. *Revelations of Divine Love,* ed. Marion Glasscoe. Exeter: University of Exeter Press, 1993.

Katterbach, Joseph, ed., Sheila Hughes, trans. *Three Mystics.* New York: 1949.
Kavanaugh, Kieran, and Otilio Rodriguez, trans. *The Collected Works of St. Teresa of Avila.* Washington: ICS Publications, 1980.

Lincoln, Victoria. *Teresa: A Woman.* Albany, N.Y.: SUNY Press, 1985.
Llewelyn, Robert. *The Joy of the Saints.* Springfield: Templegate Publishers, 1989.

Miller, Jean Baker. *Toward a New Psychology of Women.* Boston: Beacon Press, 1976.
Moore, Katherine. *She for God: Aspects of Women and Christianity.* London: Allison and Beasley, Ltd., 1978.

Noffke, Suzanne. *Catherine of Siena: The Dialogue.* New York: Paulist Press, 1980.

Peers, E. Allison. *Studies of the Spanish Mystics.* New York: Macmillan, 1927.

Porcile, Maria Teresa. "Solitude and Solidarity." *Ecumenical Review.* January 1986.

Romano, Catherine. "A Psycho-Spiritual History of Teresa of Avila: A Woman's Perspective." *Western Spirituality: Historical Roots, Ecumenical Routes.* Santa Fe, N.M., 1981.

Strehlow, Wighard, and Gottfried Hertzka. *Hildegard of Bingen's Medicine.* Santa Fe: Bear and Co., 1988.

Teresa of Avila. *The Interior Castle.* Trans. Kieran Kavanaugh and Otilio Rodriguez. New York, 1979.
———. *The Life of Teresa of Jesus, The Autobiography of St. Teresa of Avila.* Trans. E. Allison Peers. New York: Image Books, 1960.

Uhlein, Gabriele. *Meditations with Hildegard of Bingen.* Santa Fe.: Bear and Co., 1983.